PRAISE FOR *THE SIZE OF A BIRD*

Clementine's poetry is magical, raw, and real, in the best ways, and left me feeling hopeful.

Zoe Whittall, author of *The Best Kind of People*
and *Holding Still For as Long as Possible.*

Morrigan's new collection uses writing itself as an entry point insisting that what must be written include "the things that didn't quite fit into the narrative, that didn't quite make sense." Her poetics and lyric prose make room for miscalculations of excess – sometimes a present tense and sometimes the shape of desire – "the size of a bird."

nancy viva davis halifax, author of *hook.*

"Can poetry hold / the anxious thoughts of lovers?" This is only one of the many complex and gorgeous inquiries Clementine Morrigan asks in *The Size of A Bird.* Morrigan's own poetry decidedly holds anxious thoughts, yes, but also desire, and trauma and healing, uncertainty and wanting, undoing and becoming—her second collection of poetry holds all of these and more.

Amber Dawn, author of *Where the Words End
and My Body Begins* and *How Poetry Saved My Life.*

PRAISE FOR *RUPTURE*

Rupture bravely captures the emotions of trauma, pleasure and recovery. This series of poems, divided into six parts, takes the reader through the author's experiences of sexual violence, discovering her sense of self and relationships, and how she has started her journey toward healing. Although some of the poems are extremely difficult to read, Morrigan's work serves as a way for others who are dealing with similar experiences to begin to articulate some of their own pain. [...] The juxtaposition of the empowerment expressed in some of the poems and the hurt in others underscores the nuanced struggle of living with a painful history.

Shameless Magazine

Rupture is a bold, honest, and thought-provoking collection of poems and short narrative writings on female embodiment, violence against women, sexuality, and feminism. Morrigan's accessible language and intimate tone invite the reader to enter into her experiences, which range from harrowing to exhilarating. She encourages readers to appreciate the challenging journey of the woman in patriarchal culture who seeks to honour her feelings, desires, and powers and carve out a truly independent existence. Her book [...] is a work that would appeal to many women who similarly struggle to live outside of sexist conditioning and norms.

Herizons Magazine

You Cant Own the Fucking Stars

COLLECTED WRITINGS ON TRAUMA, ADDICTION,
RECOVERY, AND TRANSFORMATION
2012-2016

Clementine Morrigan

You Can't Own the Fucking Stars:
Collected Writings on Trauma, Addiction,
Recovery, and Transformation 2012-2016

By Clementine Morrigan

Published by Clementine Morrigan
Montréal, Québec

clementinemorrigan.com

ISBN 978-1-9994192-0-2

Layout and design by Jay Marquis-Manicom

Cover illustration by Tommi Parrish

For Michelle.

Table of Contents

Content

This book includes detailed writing about things which could easily be upsetting, disturbing, or triggering. Some of these things include: sexual violence, rape, childhood sexual abuse/ incest, intimate partner violence, physical assault, emotional abuse, drinking and drug use, addiction/alcoholism, self injury, suicide, psychiatric incarceration, court, police, sex/sexuality, queerphobia, biphobia, and transphobia. I trust in your capacity to make the choices that are best for you, whether that means reading at a certain time and place, or not reading at all.

Introduction

This is a collection of writing produced between the years 2012 and 2016. It is five years worth of writing which appeared in zines and online. A few of the pieces are previously unpublished. It begins with a newly sober Clementine grappling with trauma and addiction, and traces a path through months and years as I grew in my recovery. As with most of my writing there is a heavy focus on sexuality, gender, queerness, and surviving a massive amount of sexual violence. It's a record of the ways I tried to grow and heal and better understand myself, my life, and my world, during the first five years of my recovery.

At the time of compilation I am almost six years sober. My life looks completely different today than it did when I wrote these words. Reading over this writing, I am struck by how much has changed. My opinions on many things have changed. My understanding of my life and many of the stories I tell here have changed. Some of the things I understood as healthy and in line with my recovery when I wrote these pieces I now understand as harmful and a repetition of the trauma I have known all my life. In particular I was in a long term relationship during much of this writing that I wanted to believe was good and healthy, but which was actually traumatic and deeply harmful.

Change is a sign of growth. Feeling differently than I did when I wrote these words does not mean that these words hold no truth, power, or importance. In many cases I can see myself digging deep and getting so, so close to what was really happening. In every case these words are a genuine and earnest attempt to heal and make sense of my life. It is my hope that these words, imperfect as they are, will help others on their own recovery paths, that they will help to shine light and offer hope during the hard work of recovery from trauma and/or addiction. It is my hope that they will offer ways to think through gender, sexuality, trauma, shame, desire, jealousy, polyamory, relationships, addiction, recovery, sobriety, and possibility, among other things.

At the time of compilation I have different things to say about many of these topics, because my growth has continued and my healing has deepened. I have changed. These days I live in Montréal, I am happy, and I know what it means to truly be loved. I have deeply healed the split that severed me from my sexuality and I continue to do that healing work. I am living in line with my integrity and I have found ways to speak the truth, the real truth that I never wanted to look at. And as always, more will be revealed. I am excited about the ongoing process of healing and growth. My new zines series *Fucking Magic* documents what that process looks like for me today.

With love and solidarity and the deepest wishes for your deepest healing,

Clementine

2012

After the Disaster

I rub my clit at night in my bed and it feels good
I haven't fucked anybody except for myself for in more than six months and it
    feels good
I am alive with something that there are not words for
the colours are brighter and even after the disaster I am not defeated
there is always more
I have somewhere to come home to now and that somewhere is myself
I no longer search for completion inside the bottle or inside someone else
I am enough, I am good for myself
I revel in the splendor of my body, I arch my back, I squeeze my breasts
I write love poems to myself

I was sitting in the courtroom and my heart was pounding in my chest
and the jury declared him not guilty of raping me and he raised his arm in
    celebration
I felt like I was being split in half despite how prepared I was for this
there was this shiver that ran through my centre that I could not contain
the anger, the shame, the humiliation, the grief
I could not pretend that it was all okay
he was declared not guilty of what he had done and my body there on the bed
    and his cum inside me dripping down my leg

I make love to myself in the dark of my room
in the very room he raped me in, on the very bed he raped me on
my fingers explore the textures of my pussy
I pull pleasures multilayered and endless from my own depths
I come again and again and again
and each time I do the pleasure spreads throughout me
it spreads like fire through my body from my pussy through my spine into my
    heart
across every part of me he touched
every part of me he tried to own
it arrives at my brainstem and spreads throughout my brain
I remember who I am
I remember that I am my own

Six Months Sober

I am an alcoholic. I am six months sober. My sobriety is the most important thing in my life. I am so fucking grateful for my sobriety and I am committed to maintaining it. For about nine years I was in the throes of active alcoholism. It shape-shifted over time. I struggled with it. I denied it. I accepted it. I celebrated it. I was terrified of it. I couldn't stop it. I drank alone. I drank with strangers. I lost friends. I drank in alley ways, parks, bars, my living room, on public transit. In the morning, all night, in the middle of the day. I drank litres of wine, countless bottles, pints and pitchers of beer, and liquor in the early days. My hands shook. My mind wandered. I would pass the liquor store, wine store or beer store and it would start. I would think I could just go in and grab something for later and then I would and then I would start drinking it immediately. I would always eye the supply and I was never calm because I was never sure there was enough. I would get fucked up and then head into the streets looking for men to fuck. In the end I was coming to, half dressed in the middle of a heated argument, having no fucking idea where I was or who this guy was telling me to get the fuck out of his apartment and whether or not we fucked and whether or not we used a condom. It was scary. I wanted to believe I could control it. I wanted to believe I could just have a glass of wine with dinner and then I would end up getting sexually assaulted while sleeping on a park bench. Sobriety is like finally coming out of a storm. It's like finally putting my feet on dry land. I have to constantly remember and remind myself that I am an alcoholic because as an alcoholic I am fucking delusional and I can easily convince myself that I can drink normally. I convinced myself for years despite the trips in the ambulance, the hours vomiting into the toilet, the many times I was assaulted, the many things I regretted. Now I hold the knowledge of my alcoholism in my heart like a precious stone. It is the most important thing. It means I don't have to pretend anymore. It means when I pass people on the patio and I think, wouldn't it be nice to have a cold beer?, I can simply remind myself that it would not be nice, it would not be one beer, I am an alcoholic and I cannot drink. Thank the goddess that I know that now. May I never again forget it.

City Lights

I searched the city streets in the freezing cold for some illusive mystery, some intangibility, something sweet and empty that certainly would fill me. I followed the glittering of city lights and I was mesmerized by the glow. I was enchanted by a fantasy that I couldn't put my finger on let alone hold. And I took him home, held him in my arms, felt his body next to mine, searching my mind for his name, asking him again and it should be embarrassing but it's not. I remember when it was still good and I was dizzy with it and I had luck. I remember his body and his tattoos and he thought he was using me but I was using him too. I searched this city with a hunger, a pressing hunger and I ended up on some bathroom floor and I was proud and in the tangle of my body and his I felt a flash of something that almost felt real. I ended up in a stairwell with alarmed doors inside a mall and I was pissing on the floor and arguing with my boyfriend and crying my eyes out and we pushed the doors open and the alarms sounded and we ran. And I ended up alone in a park, writing nonsensical poetry into my little book and wishing, wishing I could explain this ache inside my chest that seemed forever to expand and take me deeper into an emptiness that was devouring whatever was left of whoever I am. The sidewalks were full of glitter, I sat on them and held the freezing feet of a shoeless woman in my hands, trying to warm them, telling her she was cold. I ate cheese sandwiches that the Christians gave me and I was ungrateful and swore at them and insulted their god. And I hunted. I consumed. I was tangled in sheets but there was something tangled in me, some kind of pulsing, aching question, some kind of blinding, burning pain. I had a marker and I wrote on every surface, scrawling, drunken letters that tried to explain.

I Want a Lover

I want a lover who respects me
who is not intimidated by my intelligence
or my sexual confidence
who has a personality as bold as my own
I want a lover who can fuck me sober
who will eat my pussy like it's the last meal
they'll ever have

I like sex, I like fucking
I like flirtations and I like touching
and I've had my fill in this lifetime already
right now I'm content on my own
I'm my own lover and my own best friend
in time I might just let someone else in

but I want a lover who is something special
who has a presence of their own
and doesn't try to shine off my glow
I want a lover who has something
to bring to the table
who makes love like a conversation
who takes their time
who looks into my eyes

You Can't Own the Fucking Stars

I have bigger dreams than being your wife. Bigger dreams than being the girl you're fucking tonight. There were times when I couldn't see past the fulfillment of the next fix, the next drink, the next fuck, the next bong hit. But now I can. I don't know what's on the horizon but it's as big as the ocean. I can tell you that my words are real and they are powerful and they are here for a reason. I can tell you that this body is on this earth for more than fulfilling your next fix, more than sucking your dick, more than that and more than this. And for the first time in my life I have the patience to wait and see. I forgo the fulfillment of the moment because I want to get to know me. I'm the girl of my fucking dreams. The goddess herself has her own plans for me. And I can take pleasure in myself. I can take pleasure in my own company. I can take pleasure on my bicycle as I take on the city on my own. I don't need you there correcting me and I am doing better on my own. I can take pleasure on my skateboard as I take on the hill, hit a bump and go flying through the air. And I don't need you there to reassure me I'm okay when I hit the pavement. I can take pleasure in my guitars, I don't need your opinion, you can't even put together a single chord. And I can take pleasure in my words. They tell the truth even when you try to undo it, even when you deny and silence it. I have bigger dreams than being groomed by you, bigger dreams than being your dream girl, bigger dreams than being okay by you. I don't need your approval and I don't want it either. I have outgrown you and I always was more than you could handle. You had big dreams of being my man but once you had me you got scared. You were attracted to my power and then you were threatened by it so you had to break me down, make me submissive, make me yours. But I was never yours. You can't own the fucking stars.

Stand Still

I stay with the stillness and it is endless. This is what I was afraid of. The sound of my own heartbeat, the cold air and the dark sky and no one there by my side. Just me and the moonlight. Just me and the endlessness of existence. Staring straight into the face of heaven. Staring straight into my own mind. This blood that pulses through my veins is mine. This vitality I couldn't end even though I wanted to so many times. I tried to give myself away because I was too much to handle. I tried to play myself down, play myself off, forget myself. But I was always still here, always still. I remember fucking him on his living room floor before he had any furniture in the house. I remember feeling uncertain, certain that I was a ghost. I remember trying so hard to manifest, looking in the mirror and seeing someone else. Drinking a beer as I waited in front of his house. I wanted it and what I wanted was nothing and I remember years later after everything he tried to tell me. He said, you were too good for that shit, you always were. And by then I knew it, by then I had figured it out, that I had been lying to myself, inventing happiness and sadness for the sake of it, settling for less. By then I knew it wasn't real but I pulled him into my arms anyway, let him put his weight on top of me anyway because I still couldn't stand myself, I still couldn't stand still. Now I stay with the stillness, I stare into the heavens which are endless. I listen to the sound of my pulse and I'm not frightened, not anymore. I don't need to be fucking some guy on his living room floor or some storage room floor or some bathroom floor, I don't need to be filling the emptiness with an endlessness of something less than something more. I hear the call of the goddess, her voice crackling through the electricity of energy that makes up existence in this dimension and I smile at her. I am whole. I am here and I am whole.

Pothead

I smoked multiple grams of weed every day for eight years. I smoked bongs in the morning. I loved my fuckin weed. And I knew I was an alcoholic and the alcohol was dramatic and it was clearly destroying my life. But I figured weed wasn't a problem. It was just weed. I didn't hit the bong and black out. I didn't hit the bong and destroy all my relationships. But I spent more money on weed than rent and going without it for even a couple hours left me feeling very uncomfortable and irritable. When I quit drinking this time and decided to get serious about sobriety and changing my life, I realized that smoking weed every day is not sobriety, even if I cut out the booze. So, I gave up weed. I had physical withdrawal symptoms. The concept that weed is not physically addictive is fuckin bullshit. I had zero appetite. Food made me sick. I puked after eating half a banana. I lost weight. I could not fall asleep and I have never before in my life had insomnia. These physical withdrawal symptoms were terrible and lasted about two weeks. But I got through them with the help of my local sober community. And I got sober for real. Six months with no alcohol and no weed and no other drugs. I drink coffee, that's it. I realize that, just like with alcohol, I can't be a social smoker. I can't smoke a joint every now and again. It won't work. I've crossed the line into addiction and there is no going back. I need to be sober. Now that I am sober I can see how addicted I was. Compared to my alcoholism my weed addiction never seemed like a big deal to me but it was a big deal. It totally controlled my life.

I Have Everything I Need

Everything I need is already inside of me. The goddess speaks to me. She reminds me of my divinity. I have laid myself down on the pavement. I have laid myself down on the floor. I slept in someone else's piss in the freezing cold underneath a pile of cardboard. I felt the pain and it felt me. I saw the abyss and it saw me. I engaged the madness and it engaged me. And what was I know will never be. But I have all I need. I awoke to the argument. I awoke to the fight. I fell asleep in his arms believing somehow that it would be alright. It never was and it never will be. But I have all I need. I walked in the rain, weighed down by my grief. I took the time to acknowledge it, to witness it, to let it be. I buried the box with all our photographs in it, deep within the earth and I set myself free. Because it was and it will never be. Where there were words there is only silence and where there was love there is only violence. I put the flower on the grave. I cried my tears and I walked away. I have everything I need.

2013

Asking For It

Booze and the way that I consumed it brought me places and made me someone. Not the kind of places you would want to go to or the kind of person you would want to be. Drinking brought me to alleyways, sidewalks, barrooms, stranger's apartments, snowbanks, park benches and bushes in a park. Drinking turned me into a kind of person who was read a certain way: as a drunk, a slut, a crazy person, a bitch, a girl who nobody cared about, a girl you could get away with doing anything to, a girl who was asking for it.

I was a horrible drunk, an obnoxious drunk, an ugly drunk, a loud drunk. I was a mean drunk, a slutty drunk, a pathetic drunk. I got kicked out of bars, thrown face first off a streetcar, punched in the face, sexually assaulted, GHB'd. I got a knife pressed up to my stomach, a condom taken off without permission, a bag of ice on my head.

Booze was an oblivion that called me endlessly. It created a world of chaos, a world where the only point of reference was a bottle. I felt perpetually unsafe to the point where feeling unsafe felt natural. It was my way of being. I was assaulted regularly and in the back of my mind I blamed myself because I was the one with the big mouth, the one asleep on the park bench, the one making a scene. I was 'asking for it'. And I got it in plenty.

Booze and the way that I consumed it created a reality for me and those around me. There are narratives about girls like me, what we are, what we deserve, what happens to us. It is an accepted 'truth' that girls who put themselves in such dangerous situations are at least partially responsible for the bad things that then happen to them. This was a 'truth' written on my body and although it made me angry it was a truth that I also believed.

I rebelled against it by drinking more and by telling myself that I didn't care. Violence was a language that I came to know quite well. I was crazy. I acted fucking crazy. And my craziness made me a target and simultaneously protected me. I told myself that this was a way of being that I needed and loved and that I chose freely. I told myself that this oblivion was the only thing keeping me alive and that the violence was an unpleasant side effect. An unfortunate but inevitable consequence to my chosen and beloved lifestyle.

Sometimes it slipped through the cracks of my denial that I was an alcoholic but I could not face the powerlessness of my addiction because my consumption was the only thing that gave me any power. I had control over something. I had control over the fact that I could always have more.

Now, booze and the ways I consumed it bring me to different places and make me a different person. My recovery brings me to church basements, community centres and coffee shops. My recovery makes me into the kind of person that people say things to like 'good for you'.

Those who aren't alcoholics themselves and who don't know me from before say things like 'are you sure you're really an alcoholic?' and 'I'm sure you'll be able to drink again in the future' because they have no idea about the way that I drank and where it took me. They cannot even begin to conceive of what my reality used to look like. Other sober alcoholics don't say things like that because they know.

I am eternally grateful for my sobriety and I know that without it I would still be experiencing violence on a regular basis. Yet this does not mean that I believe I was responsible for the violence that happened to me or deserving of it. Regardless of how fucked up I was acting, no one has the right to do the things that have been done to me. No one has the right to drag me down the stairs, pull a knife on me, grab my ass while I am asleep, put GHB in my drink, throw me off a streetcar, punch me in the face, touch my breasts without consent, pull my shirt down, throw me into a wall, smash my face with a weighted object. No one has the right to do that shit to anyone, drunk or not, addict or not. Drunks are still human beings. There is no such thing as 'asking for it'.

While in active alcoholism I remember how strange any attempt at living a normal life felt. I remember the fear I felt that anyone might recognize me while I was sober and trying to act normal from one of my consistent drunken rampages. And now that I am in recovery it happens still, people recognize me from before. They remember the fucked up girl with unfocused eyes screaming and getting kicked off the salvation army van. They look at me now, acting normal, speaking clearly and they cannot believe that it is the same person.

But it is. That was me. So is this.

Rewiring My Brain by Making Different Choices

Last night I had a severe episode of depression. It's hard to explain. But it's not an unfamiliar experience for me. I've been having these episodes for about twelve years. Basically, a whole cluster of negative thought patterns, feelings of hopelessness, worthlessness and despair, inability to see new possibilities and new routes, overwhelming circumstances and emotions come together and crash into each other. At that point, I feel like I am going to explode. I feel literally like I am going to explode. The feelings in me are so intense that I feel I absolutely must relieve them but I have simultaneously convinced myself that there is no way out, there is no new possibility, no new option. I am so intensely uncomfortable and in so much pain and I feel absolutely helpless to do anything about it. These states started developing for me when I was fourteen. The depression I had been feeling for several years already became unmanageable in the ways I have just described. It became so intense that I became compelled to do something about it while in a mind state that nothing can be done. This led me to seek immediate relief in self destructive ways: originally I went to cutting myself, later in life I went to getting drunk. These releases worked. But their ability to address my distress became less with time. So my cutting became more severe and took up more and more of my body. My alcohol intake increased and increased and then, simply drinking huge amounts wasn't enough. I needed more than that. So my behaviour while drunk was a continuation of that seeking of relief: I found some random person to have sex with or I became violent, emotionally and/or physically and sometimes no matter what I did I could not find the relief and I would end up crying and freaking out, which was what I did when I was fourteen before I found cutting and drinking.

Last night it happened. All the feelings crashed into each other and I was so overwhelmed. I started crying my eyes out. I felt that pressure inside of myself and I needed relief. Visually, in my mind, graphic images of cutting myself revealed themselves to me. My skin had that feeling of being too full and wanting to be split open. The oblivion of alcohol called to me. I just needed to stop feeling the way I was feeling. But all my coping strategies were closed to me. I have decided not to cut myself and not to drink. So how am I supposed to deal with the emotions? While this experience of severe depression is very familiar to me, my response to it was not. Instead of seeking immediate relief, I just stayed with it. I tried distracting myself with TV, but that did not work. So there I was, me and this clawing, bursting, terrible hopeless intensity. I cried my fucking eyes out. I called helplines. The first one I got through to there was a man on the end of the line. I didn't want to talk to a man but I did anyway. He was not helpful. He just kept saying "everything will be okay" and telling me I'm too young to feel this way, that I have my whole life ahead of me. But I still vented to him. I wailed and cried and told him exactly how hopeless and devastated I was feeling. He hung up on me.

I had called the rape crisis line and was still waiting for a call back. The feelings were not relenting. They were intensifying. I took a shower and sat in the hot water bawling my eyes out. Then I turned it to freezing cold and stood under the freezing water feeling somewhat calmed by an intensity that was outside of myself. But the crying would not let up. I prayed. I begged the goddess to help me. I told her point blank that I can't continue living feeling this way and I need her help. Then I dragged myself out of the shower and into bed still crying my eyes out. The phone rang and it was the rape crisis line calling me back. The voice on the other end was a woman and she sounded calm and wise. She listened to me. She did not tell me everything is going to be okay. She told me things are going to be rough. She told me it is going to take time and I can't expect myself to just snap out of these feelings. She told me it's okay to cry and to feel sad but that it's not okay to feel despair. She told me to tell myself "I want to feel calm. I don't want to feel desperate." She told me it's normal for me to feel empty right now because I am changing, I am coming back to myself, maybe for the first time, I may never have been with myself before. She told me to try not to take myself for granted, that so many women did. She told me I deserve to feel better, that I am worth going through this pain to see what is on the other side. She told me that my feeling that I had only ever been truly happy with my abusive ex was normal, and that it wasn't love I felt with him but the comfort of feeling accepted and like I belong somewhere, something I may not have felt at any other time. She told me to take it one day at a time. That's all I have to do. And to try to eat and rest and shower and to stay sober and stay true to myself. She told me not to take on other people's negativity and focus on myself. She knew without me saying so that I would be upset about my puffy eyes in the morning. She told me to put a cool cloth over my eyes and that puffy eyes aren't the end of the world.

I felt calm. And tired. We said goodbye. I took an Advil and put a cool cloth over my eyes and went to sleep. I feel that the goddess spoke to me and answered my prayer through that woman. And for the first time in many, many years, I experienced an episode of depression all the way through. I cried and cried and prayed and talked it out but I did not seek escape through alcohol, drugs, sex or self injury. And I survived it. And what I realized today is that these episodes of depression that I get may be the distress my mind experiences as it goes through major changes, as it shifts from one way of being to another. My brain knows that it can't live with the way things are, so I begin to make changes, but then my brain freaks out because it does not know what to expect. Instead of just riding through the discomfort, holding out to see what is on the other side, I always revert back to my old ways, halting the progression and ensuring future episodes of the same thing as my brain attempts the transition. I am not going to be who I've been anymore. I am rewiring my brain by making different choices and the results of these new choices are bringing me into realms of new possibilities. I do not have to repeat the same cycle over and over again and I am not going to anymore.

Too Crazy for Healthcare?

I haven't had a family doctor for ten years or so. I've basically patched together healthcare using appointments at planned parenthood. I really need to get a doctor so that I can be dealing with the same person and so that I can get more comprehensive healthcare. Doctors, as you may know, are pretty hard to come by. I recently found a local doctor who is accepting patients and I made an appointment with her.

At the intake appointment she asked me general questions about my health and history. I was honest with her that I am a recovering alcoholic and it came up that I've been in psych wards when I was a teenager. Her demeanor became ruder and ruder as the appointment went on. She told me that she wouldn't be my doctor unless I saw a psychiatrist, because she believed all aspects of my health need to be attended to. I told her I'm in counseling for my trauma and I'm in a 12 step program to address my alcoholism. I need a doctor to address my physical health.

She told me that I need a psychiatrist, that I need to consider medication and that the only psychiatrists who would see me, because of my 'history of overlapping mood issues and addiction', were at CAMH. I told her that I was willing to see a psychiatrist but that I was unwilling to go on medication, and that I was skeptical about CAMH because I have heard bad things. She repeated herself that I need a psychiatrist and that the ones at CAMH were the only ones who would see me and stated that I would probably need medication because I'd been self medicating with alcohol. She then abruptly got up and started leaving the room saying 'this is not a good fit'. She refused to be my doctor.

Because I don't want to go to CAMH and be medicated I was denied healthcare. I need a pap smear and blood work, crazy or not. And she is withholding that basic healthcare until I consent to go to CAMH. That is discrimination. My alcoholism and psychiatric history have nothing to do with my need for cancer screening and basic healthcare. Because I don't agree with her interpretation of my needs (after having met me for five minutes) I am denied the basic healthcare that I need. What the fuck.

All over the city of Toronto there is graffiti that reads 'CAMH is killing the sick', 'CAMH is killing the poor' and 'CAMH client rights a joke'. I notice this graffiti and I listen to it. 'Crazy' people deserve a voice and we deserve to be listened to and heard. We do not need our experiences defined for us. I think it's fucked that a doctor who denies me healthcare and ignores the blatant criticisms that CAMH is harming patients can present herself as acting in the interest of my health. Is the goal my health, or is it my compliance?

Beginning Again

In 2005, about a year into active alcoholism and addiction, I put out the first issue of my perzine *licking stars off ceilings*. About a year later I put out the second issue and started writing under the name 'Clementine Cannibal.' By 2012 I had put out twenty three issues of *licking stars off ceilings*. It was a zine that explored and glamourized my drunken exploits, the random sex I had, the ravaging sadness and rage and pain that ruled my life. I created a persona for myself. I hid behind an armour of rage. I tried very hard to convince myself and everyone else that I didn't give a fuck. I had been hurt so many times. I believed that trying to be a good person made me weak. My existence was a blur of alcohol and drugs. I drowned everything out. I abandoned all of the morals and ethics that had previously been so important to me. I just wanted to drink and fuck and I would start fights with anyone, any time, for no reason at all. I slowly and steadily became a hateful person and in my zine I tried to make it all look cool. I remember once a zinester wrote to me and said she was worried about me. I was so angry. How dare she. I wanted to be wild and free and I thought I was but I was chained to addiction, I was obliterated by pain, I had completely lost myself.

Sometimes I feel a lot of regret about *licking stars off ceilings* and the 'Clementine Cannibal' persona I created. I hate the fact that I tried to make it cool not to give a fuck. Because the truth is I give so many fucks. I care deeply. I hate the fact that I glamourized addiction instead of being honest about the way it was destroying my life. I hate the fact that I turned myself into a two dimensional caricature, that I threw out my values, that I was mean to people, that I used people, that I was just disrespectful to myself and the world and that I acted like that was a really cool way to be. At the same time, as fucked up as a lot of my zines were, they were also pretty much the only healthy thing in my life. The hours spent writing, cutting and pasting, photocopying, collating and sending out zines were a lifeline. They were a small space in which I cared about more than oblivion, even though I was writing about and glamourizing the oblivion. The connections I made with other zinesters started to remind me who I was, started to reconnect me with my values and I made some friends who are still in my life today. Those zines expressed where I was at for about nine years of my life: a dishonest, hurting, angry, vengeful, nihilistic and sad place. Underneath all of that was the spark, the longing, the part of me that can't be destroyed, that compelled me to keep writing, keep expressing, and it is that spark that kept me alive, although I could have died, many times.

I want to come clean about all of this stuff. I want to be honest about the messy and painful journey that my life has been. I am nineteen months sober at the time of writing this and I am finally far enough away from that life to be able to write about it with humility and honesty. I feel that telling the truth is the only way to set things right. I want to say that addiction is not cool and is not fun. It was a horrible, miserable, lonely existence. I want to say that 'not giving a fuck' never stopped me from secretly giving a fuck. I want to say that I am not a fucking cannibal. I'm a vegetarian and have been since I was six years old. I want to say that I am sorry. I am sorry that I presented a fake persona, that I hurt people during those years when my best friend was always a bottle and that I am doing my best at this point in my life to be accountable and to live with honesty and kindness and compassion and humility. I am ready to start writing a perzine again and it will be different than the zines I made before. I write this zine explicitly from a place of love. I write this zine from a place of awareness that I need other people. I write this zine from a place of courage and hope. I write this zine because I want to tell a different story.

Maybe

Maybe it's simple. Maybe I could try. Maybe it will get better. Maybe I should try. Maybe I am not the worst of me. Maybe I am not going to be alone forever. Maybe there is something else, something more. Maybe I could try. Maybe it is easy. Maybe there is help. Maybe I am loved. Maybe I could be loved. Maybe it doesn't have to be like this. Maybe it won't be this way forever. Maybe there's a way out. Maybe I don't have to live like this. Maybe there is another way. Maybe I don't need the alcohol. Maybe I don't need the drugs. Maybe I never needed him. Maybe I will be okay. Goddess, maybe it could be okay.

Seven Gates

Through seven gates I pass. At each one I let go of some false pride, some attachment that I confuse with who I am. Carefully, each careful construction that I have crafted is laid bare and discarded. I must go deep. I must not settle for self-help and feeling better. I must not rely on good days and better weather. I must dare the deep. The depths which call to me. The great below, where beneath, lays hidden all that I would hide. I must dare to go there and there, I must dare to die.

Rebirth is not an easy task but it is the only thing to do. When the games you have been playing are more than boring you. When one more time would kill you and what's worse, you know deep down that you really don't want to die. Rebirth is messy. It is a terrifying journey. One in which you do not predict the outcome. You do not know what will be revived, who you will be when you return from the other side.

But I go. I strip myself of everything I've worn. I lay down the lies and the solemn declarations that yes, this, is who I am. I lay down my grievances, my victories, my wild stories, my clever renditions of truth, my sadness, my intelligence, my strength and my ability to do it all alone. I lay down my victimhood, my mental illness, my troubled ways, my feminism, my ghost stories, my aching heart, my poetry. I lay down my love, my inability to love, my fear, my regret, my shame. I lay down my anger, my this-I-will-never-forgive, my certainty and my blame. I lay down the memories which I have worn like scarves, wrapped around my neck like nooses, my scars which I have worn like bracelets, my crowning achievement: ruin.

And it is not that these things will be gone forever, obliterated into a nothingness from which they cannot return, it is that they may be. It is only in daring to surrender them, in loosening my grip and letting go of them, that I can be reborn. I do not know what shapes will form when I emerge from down below. I do not know what will come back up with me, what will have changed, what will have merged, what will have burned. I do not know if I will even be who I am anymore but still, I let go.

Desolation

When the drive to live has no space to move in it turns inward, it becomes inverted, it becomes a drive for death. I was forbidden to say the things I knew. I was ashamed to be alive. I was so afraid of everything but most of all I hated myself for being so afraid, so unable to just be normal. I hated the secrets which I couldn't even say to myself. I hated the truth which was too awful to say. I hated not being safe. I hated the helplessness of childhood, the powerlessness. I hated that my 'no' was punished and silenced. I hated the slow and painful process of becoming good. A good girl. I loved being bad but I hated the rejection that came with it. I just wanted to rest in love and I knew that meant giving up my drive to live, it meant submission. So I submitted. I let it happen. I lost myself. I gave myself up.

When I found the bottle I found the buried rage. I found all those things I could never say. The force of that drive to live was translated into utter destruction, desolation. I would destroy myself. My self-destruction was a loving declaration. It was the only way I knew how to own myself. To kill myself meant that I was mine to kill. To scream and to say the unsayable things, to sit on the ground, rocking back and forth and pulling out my hair. To tell the sick secrets, spit them out on the sidewalk, to say them over and over again, a broken record, an endless consumption, a compulsion, an obsession, an overflowing, bloody mess.

Don't fucking touch me, don't fucking touch me, don't fucking touch me.

My body makes me sick so I am not it. It is a thing I have learned to manipulate. Oh god I hate being alive. I feel nothing and I hate to feel nothing and I hate to feel anything and I hate myself so much. I hate this flesh that is invaded. I hate the weakness, the sickness, the rush of pleasure, the sickening desire. I hate everything about it. I just want to be disembodied thoughts, I just want the safety of floating miles and miles away.

So I went to war with my body. I learned to turn it into dead matter, to make it into raw material, it would not be who I am. I manipulated it like a puppet, pulling strings to make it move. It would not destroy me, no. I would learn how to use it. Since this sick flesh-mess is what I have been told that I am, since these doors have already been broken, since these walls have already been smashed in, since I cannot escape it, since my poetry doesn't keep my body from being touched anyway, I learned to use it. I learned how to use it like a coin, I traded it for something better, the company of someone other than myself.

I realize that he is fucking me and I can't feel anything, over and over and over and over and over again. I can't feel anything. I hate the sounds, hate the light. I hate him. I hate myself. I am sick with hate and the only relief I will have is the oblivion that shuts off the voice in my head that knows how much I hate this, the oblivion that turns me back into an animal, a child, a storm, that turns me into some other form, some other thing that I think I was before. I drank the heat inside the bottle, split and spilled and spoiled all that is and was. I made the unbearable something I could bear. I made the unknowable something I could know. I made the unlivable something I could live. I made use of that deadened drive to live.

Face in the toilet bowl, puking my guts out, unable to even think, my pulse in my head so fucking loud, just trying to get the poison out of me. If only I could vomit it all up, everything that happened, every sick violation, if only these regular morning rituals of throwing up the contents of my stomach would really make me new again. If only the oblivion would really let me forget. If only the momentary relief from the fear did not multiply into a magnitude of terror. If only I could face myself. If only I could entertain the thought, for only a moment, that I am worthy of love.

Down to Fuck and Not So Down to Fuck: On Consent, Communication, Trauma and Power within 'Sex-Positive' Politics

I am a rape survivor and a domestic violence survivor and a sexual assault survivor and a childhood sexual abuse survivor and I am a woman who lives in a culture of sexual violence and has to live my life under the threat and reality of sexual harassment, objectification, sexual abuse and sexism every day. I have post-traumatic stress disorder as a result of all of this and part of the way that manifests for me is that when I get scared and I know that fighting and fleeing are not realistic options (or options I can imagine as real), I freeze. I dissociate from my body so that when the assault happens I will not be as present for it. This is a survival tactic that I learned at a young age and it has helped me a lot. But the fact is, I am sick of being assaulted, I am sick of unwanted and traumatizing sexual contact, and I have been trying very hard to work on my communication skills, to work on setting and keeping boundaries, to work on saying 'no' and telling my lovers clearly what I want and don't want. It is difficult, exhausting work. And unfortunately not as successful as I would like it to be.

He is touching my breasts and I feel like dead flesh. I feel a million miles away. In my mind I command him to stop but my mouth won't move to form the words, my body is frozen stiff. I don't move at all but I tense my body away from him. I want him to get the message. I have already told him so many times that I am a survivor, that I have PTSD, that it is hard for me to say no. I wish desperately that my complete lack of response will signal to him that I am not interested in his hard dick pressed against my back. But he doesn't stop. I can't believe this is happening again. When his fingers brush my nipples I feel a rising of sexual response and I want to throw up. This body is alien to me. I am not a part of it. I don't want this, don't want to be turned on, don't want to fuck, just want to go back to sleep like I was doing before he decided that he was turned on and wanted to fuck me.

I am a feminist, a sex-positive feminist, although the hollowness of that term is becoming more and more evident as sexual assaults go on at sex-positive events, as my critique that the mainstream 'barely-legal' porn I found in my ex-boyfriend's room was sexist was met with a baffled response because I'm supposed to be pro-porn. And I am pro-porn but porn does not exist in a magical vacuum, in some mythical place where sexual violence doesn't happen, where child abuse doesn't happen, where coercion doesn't happen, where women are not endlessly sexually objectified. I have nothing but respect for sex workers and my critique was not of them when I called that porn sexist. My critique is of a culture of sexual violence that eroticizes a lack of consent, hence the term 'barely-legal', she is barely of an age of legal consent and in a rape culture that is fucking sexy.

I am a feminist who loves sex, who works hard to live my sexual life freely, fucking without shame. I am a woman who as a child was taught that sex is dangerous and bad and who wanted to discover it as otherwise and so had lots and lots of it, paid and unpaid, with lovers and strangers and with myself, on mattresses on floors in empty apartments, with long terms partners, in parks and alleyways, drunk and sober, with toys and without them, with women, men and other people, kinky and not so kinky and extremely kinky, intimate and romantic, friends with benefits, no strings attached, anonymous and a lot of it was good and pleasurable and a lot of it was mediocre and lacked good communication and a lot of it was traumatizing too. And I have to say, though I shouldn't have to say it, that no, it wasn't the anonymous, paid or random sex that was always traumatizing and the indoor, monogamous, intimate sex that was always good. That's bullshit and not my truth at all. I was raped by my long-term boyfriend who I lived with, I came like crazy with clients, I had really good sex in a university classroom and really bad sex on a one-year ever-so-romantic anniversary. I also had a one-night-stand pull the condom off without permission and long term partners pressure me into unprotected sex. What I am trying to say is that whether sex is good or bad, healthy or unhealthy has nothing to do with whether it is sanctioned by the state and by society as normal and healthy and good and right. It has everything to with honesty and communication, both verbal and non-verbal; it has everything to do with respect.

But good communication and honesty and honest respect are unfortunately harder to come by than they should be. Unfortunately this sex-positive culture that has begun to lift female pleasure and desire, queer sex, kink, sex work and many other sexual practices from the depths of shame and silence that they have been buried in, has done little to address the realities of power and violence in our lives. Sex is good. Yes, it can be. It is nothing to be ashamed of and yes, that still unfortunately needs to be said. The culture of sexual shame has not yet been completely lifted and so therefore sex-positive work is still very important. But this work needs to become far more nuanced. We need to get beyond 'sex is good.' We need to acknowledge that sex can be good, amazing, healthy and wonderful and that it is also frequently unwanted, coercive, and manipulative. We need to acknowledge, consider, explore and work with the reality that sex takes place within systems of power like sexism, queerphobia, rape culture, white supremacy, colonialism, transphobia, ableism, whorephobia and others. We need to acknowledge that people come to sexual experiences with different access to power, different histories and different realities. We need to recognize that while 'consent is sexy' saying no is a privilege that has been long-denied to many of us and that we are not going to just wake up one day being able to say no and mean it when that no has been punished and silenced in us all our lives.

Consent is about more than 'yes' and 'no.' Communication is not just verbal. We need to pay attention to each other, be considerate of each other, be honest with each other and we need to respect each other.

Too often my body is a dead thing and my lover doesn't care. Too often my need to stop is met with subtle annoyance. Too often both my 'yes' and my 'no' are shamed. The solution to a culture that shames me for any sexual desire is not to create culture in which I am shamed when I don't have sexual desire. People who want to fuck all the time are not more or less liberated than people who don't want to fuck some or all of the time. There is nothing inherently better about having lots of sex than there is about having no sex or some sex. Just because I have an extensive sexual history does not mean that my body is always sexually available to you. Just because my politics state that people should be free to fuck on their own terms, whenever and however they want, does not mean that I want to fuck you right now.

My trauma and my history of surviving sexual violence, my need to stop, my desire not to have sex, does not make me a bad sex-positive feminist. My analysis of sexism and the violent and oppressive structures under which much sex takes place does not make me anti-sex. Just because I am a proud slut, a queer poly kinky whore, does not mean that I want to fuck you right now. Just because I cannot find the words to say 'no' does not mean that I have said 'yes.' Consent is more than sexy. It is necessary. Please listen to your lovers, not just what we say verbally but also our body language, not just what we are saying in this moment but also the other things we have shared with you about our abilities to communicate during sex. Please take into consideration the histories of violence that may be in our lives, please take into consideration the systems of oppression and power that may be shaping and limiting our options and please slow it down enough to pay attention. Communicate. Be honest. And show respect.

As communities, in our bedrooms, with our lovers and fuck buddies, our friends and clients, at our sex-parties and sex-positive events, in our discussions about how hot porn can be, in the alley way, park, sex-store, around the coffee table as we discuss our sexuality with friends, in our political work and our art, we need more dialogue about all of this. We need to do more than free sex from being bad; we also need to free it from being one-dimensional and simple. We need to create space within sex for our whole selves, as survivors, as people with complex histories, as people who live with and under systems of violence and oppression, as people who may want and need different things at different times.

I Don't Want to Kill My Rapist

Being assaulted is horrible and how we choose to react to and cope with being assaulted is, I believe, deeply personal. I do not believe it is my place to judge or evaluate how someone else deals with being assaulted. So what I am about to share is about my feelings about my experiences of being assaulted.

I have been assaulted many times, both physically and sexually. When I first came into consciousness as a survivor, when I first realized that the sexual abuse I experienced as a child was, in fact, wrong as I had suspected, my reaction was rage. When I was then assaulted again, in other contexts, in my teenage and adult life, my rage multiplied. I was so angry and underneath that anger was a deep sense of helplessness. The shame and humiliation and horror of being unable to protect myself made me feel sick. In order to gain some sense of power, I wrapped myself up in an armour of rage.

I used to gain a lot of solace from slogans like "dead men don't rape", "kill your rapist", "bash back" and so on. The idea of violently seeking retribution appealed to me. The idea that I could even the scales made me feel less helpless, less violated. I glorified my rage, I projected a "don't fuck with me" attitude, I acted like I didn't give a fuck. I put on a show, I created a persona, I wanted to be just as tough, just as hard, just as powerful as the people who had hurt me. I wanted everyone to know that I was not a victim, I wanted everyone to believe that I was dangerous, tough as nails, not someone you wanted to fuck with.

None of that protected me. None of that stopped me from being assaulted again. What it did was prevent me from being honest with myself and others about the true ways that I felt about being assaulted. What it did was magnify my shame at being helpless. What it did was bury the grief and terror and fear and heartbreak and trauma and even honest anger under a fake persona. And worst of all, what it did was make me look up to my perpetrators; it made me internalize their value systems, it made me think I had to win at their game.

When I was on the floor being kicked in the stomach I just tried to protect my organs as best I could and screamed out apologies in the hopes that he would stop. That was all I could do. There was no way that I could fight this guy who was bigger and stronger and far more trained in violence than I am. There was no way that I could in fact "kill my rapist". What I did was submit and because I had internalized the belief that I had to be big and strong and tough and not take any fucking shit, this made me feel like a disgusting failure. As time has passed and I have worked on my healing I now see that my submission was a careful strategy of survival that kept me alive.

I have come to realize that not only will I never be as big and strong and as good at violence as the men who have assaulted me, I have also come to realize that I don't want to be. I don't want to kill my rapist. I don't want to bash back. I don't want to fight violence with violence. I do not want to win at their game.

As I have worked through my trauma, peeling back layer after painful layer, I have learned a lot about myself. I have learned that I am in fact a pacifist. I do not like violence. I do not want anyone to ever be assaulted ever again and that includes my rapist and the people who have violently assaulted me. I do not wish them the pain that they caused me. I do not wish them any pain at all. And when I finally admitted that to myself I found that it was far more empowering than any of the false bravado I was using to protect myself before.

I do not want to internalize a violent masculinity and call that my empowerment. I want to admit, honestly, that being assaulted is a horrifying experience, that it makes me feel weak and helpless, that it makes me feel violated, that I have feared for my life. I want to admit that I have cried and felt sick about it, that it has affected me deeply. I want to admit that I have felt fear and pain and shame. I want to admit that I am a vulnerable human being like every other human being, that I am made of flesh and blood, that I can be hurt, that I can be killed.

I am not saying that I don't believe in self-defense. I will try to defend myself if I have to and if I think it will work; although in my experience, fighting back is not even the most practical strategy for lessening the violence that is happening to me. What I am saying is that I do not want to celebrate or glorify violence.

I do not want to react to violence with more violence, even if that violence is rhetorical. I don't want to glorify violence in any way. Saying that I do not wish harm or retribution against my perpetrators does not mean that I am not holding them accountable or that I am okay with violence. Just the opposite. Saying that I do not wish harm on my perpetrators means that I don't want to become them. No matter how horrible what they did to me was, I will no longer take part in the perpetuation of violence.

I do not believe in violence. That is my truth. And I am finally at a place where I can stand by that truth and feel powerful and strong. I will not let my perpetrators take that from me.

The Girl I Used to Be

For years I pretended I wasn't a poet. I chased the sparkle of reflected light and refused to dig in the dirt. I drank wine in the cold snow and sought the warmth of human flesh not caring whose flesh it was. For years I pretended to love. I couldn't love. I had no heart to give. My heart was hiding in the earth. My heart was safe in the earth. For years I betrayed myself and anyone else I could. Having beliefs, convictions, hopes or dreams was too dangerous. Telling the truth was too dangerous. It was better to lie. For years I flirted with death, I explored the edges that separated me from some deeper oblivion, I imagined my own annihilation. I was too afraid to live. I was too afraid to feel. I didn't dare love. Lying on a mattress on the floor of a dirty apartment I stared at the ceiling and I tried to feel something. Lying to myself, chasing ghosts and shadows, never knowing what I was running from, afraid to run. For years I acted like I didn't care when I really longed for love.

We are lying in his bed and he is looking at the X-ed out heart tattoo on my wrist. He asks me what it means again. I tell him that "It used to mean don't be ruined by love, don't let it own you" and he says "Used to? What does it mean now?" and I say "It's a tribute to the sad and angry and hurting girl I used to be."

Relentless Hope

I am still in shock at what my life is now. Sometimes I really can't believe who I have become, who I'm becoming. Under all those layers of hardened fear and hate, this person was still here. Recovery, literally meaning the retrieval of that which has been lost, my own goddess-given self, my own being. It is strange and wonderful and sometimes terrifying getting to know myself again. Each day of this journey of recovery has been something new. I learn so much all the time. I lose so much all the time. I let go of so much and what I have gained in return is so much more than I could have imagined.

Being vulnerable is scary. Being open is scary. Admitting that I have seriously fucked up is scary. Looking someone in the eye is scary. Admitting that I don't know is scary. Telling the truth is scary. Letting people in is scary. Surrender is scary. But it's so good. It is so humbling. It is so relieving. It is so powerful. It is so beautiful. I am a part of this universe, not more than it and not less than it, not separate from it. I don't do any of this alone and I am never alone and I am a part of all of this. Thank you for my sobriety, thank you, thank you, thank you.

I see the sky in all its shades. I love my friends with a simple purity. I speak my truth. I am learning. I ask for help. I stop to run my fingers across the texture of tree bark. I remember to eat. I light my candles and pray. I write. I face my demons and look at the things I am so afraid to look at. I meet new people. I grow closer to the ones that I love. I act with kindness. I meditate on compassion, asking it to inform my every action. I am working to live with integrity, to integrate all of who I am, to live with wholeness. I am happy. To say those simple words and mean it in the easiest, most natural way, is more than I could have dreamed. I didn't know this life was possible.

I am writing about this because I want you to know. It is never too late. Your path will be different than mine. Your struggles and challenges will be different than mine. But I want you to know that for a long, long time I could never have imagined the life that I now have. I have contemplated and attempted suicide. I have drank myself into nothingness. I have hated myself. I have done things that made me feel great shame, things I thought I could never come back from. I believe that there is a way back for all of us. There is a way.

Now I love myself tenderly and will great courage. Now I love life with awe and humility. Now I love my friends honestly and deeply. Now I love my former enemies with endless compassion. Now I love strangers with everything that I am. Love is the guiding force in my life. My heart is too big to fit in my ribcage. I am every day humbled by this universe that I am a part of. I am every day awed by all the love and beauty in the world. I am every day inspired and encouraged and driven by a relentless hope. There is hope for you too.

Surrender

I am a writer at a loss for words. I am baffled at the way the universe works. Surrender is the best thing that has ever happened to me. I surrender every single day. I no longer know. I no longer try to run the show. It isn't mine to run. I move forward with faith. My heart is a brilliant light, my heart is a million pieces, my heart is an overused metaphor, my heart has taken me to the strangest places, the most dangerous places, my heart still secretly believed, my heart was numb so I kept on smashing it, trying to break it open.

I am shy and brave. I am here in this comfortable place. I feel safe. I look at you with new eyes. I am full of glitter like a deep dark sky outside of the limits of the city. I am looking at you with new eyes and I love what I am feeling, I love. Surrender is my favourite thing. I do it every day. Surrender brought me here. I could never have dreamed this up. I could never have designed this. I am shy and I am brave. I am full and I am seeking. I am curious and I am happy and I am overloaded with feeling. I am alive. I can't believe that I am alive, that I lived to live this.

I never want the numbness again. I never want touch without meaning. I never want motion without feeling. You say my name and you pull me back into this moment and I remember who you are, who I'm with, who I am, what year it is. You say my name and I remember that I don't have to be anybody other than who I am, that I don't need to pretend. I bury my face into your chest, pulling you so close to me, breathing you in. You are my best friend. All those conversations, all those moments, we never knew that we would end up here.

We seek a language that evades us. We wear words that fit so loose. We finally sigh, throwing up our hands, we let the words drop, fall, crash into a billion glittering shards which shine and catch the light like little stars, guiding our way through the darkness of this unknown. It doesn't matter that there aren't words. In the darkness I feel the shapes that make up your body. Your eyes are a question and I bite your shoulder, answering them.

I swallow my pride. I drink it like I have been without water for weeks. I never want to know it all. I never want to not need anyone. I never want to be sure. I only want to be here. I never want to plan it all out. I never want to pin it all down. I never want you to be anyone except for who you are. I just want to be here, right now, I just want to be here. I kiss your lips and I have never before kissed anyone who knows me like you know me.

Life is a mystery. Life is such a strange and beautiful mystery.

Self-forgiveness and Daring to Change

Recently I had the opportunity to see Sunny Drake's funny, touching and powerful *Transgender Seeking*. There are many things I could write about this incredible performance but I would like to focus on one small part that really stood out to me. Sunny's character Jimmy talks about being afraid to admit to his part in a relationship that ended badly, afraid to admit the things he had done that weren't the kindest, most mature or most respectful, afraid to admit where he fucked up, out of fear of being listed on the ominous 'bad person list'. Yet, as Jimmy reflected on this fear, he recognized that it was limiting his growth as a person. To grow, to change, to heal, to do better, he needed to be able to look at his fuck ups honestly.

This really spoke to me. As an alcoholic and addict in recovery, as a traumatized and for a long time deeply troubled person, when I got sober I looked at my past with anxiety, fear, remorse, even terror. As a feminist and queer, as a member of communities who are invested in anti-oppressive, respectful and accountable behaviour, it can be terrifying to admit the places that I have fucked up, the places I have caused harm, the mistakes I have made. Like Jimmy, no one wants to be forever listed on the 'bad person list'. Yet, also like Jimmy, I see that defensiveness and fear are not good ingredients for the making of healing and growth.

In my recovery, I have done a lot of work on making healthier choices, living with more integrity and acting in the world in a way that is grounded in my spiritual beliefs. Yet, I can't go back in time and take back all the actions in my past that were unhealthy, unkind, unconscious, defensive, hurtful and definitely not grounded in a spiritual way of being. There were times in my early recovery where I seriously contemplated suicide because of this. I despaired deeply. I thought, does any good I do now even matter, when I know that I have caused harm in the past? What is the point?

After more sobriety, lots of spiritual contemplation, lots of listening and seeking good counsel, and lots of living according to my sense of ethics, morals and spiritual truth in the here and now, I have come to see that there is a point. The point is that I am a human being. I am not perfect. I am not infallible. I do not deserve to be punished for my past nor is my life no longer worth living. The point is that I, like most of us, have fucked up, and that I can now, through my pursuit of conscious, connected and accountable living, learn from my mistakes, make better choices and pass on the things I have learned.

Daring to look honestly at one's life, daring to see where we have fucked up and daring to make real changes are powerful choices that can have a ripple effect throughout the consciousness of the universe. Daring to uproot the punishing, prison mentality that says we are defined by our worst moments and the capitalist notion that our lives are commodities which should be discarded after damage can free us to love and to love and to try again.

Forgiveness of others came much easier to me than forgiveness of self. Even the people who physically and sexually assaulted me are not permanently and irrevocably 'evil' in my mind. I do not wish them harm, only healing. I do not want them to come near me but I do not want them to disappear off of the planet either. Truly, from the bottom of my heart, I wish them love. I understand that they have been harmed by the violent culture in which we live and they have responded by creating more violence. As tragic as it is, it is not unthinkable. It is not beyond my comprehension or forgiveness.

Yet for myself, for my own wrongs, I could see no forgiveness. I thought: but I have been victimized, but I am a feminist, so I should know better. The process of self-forgiveness has taught me the greatest lesson of all: humility. I am no better and no worse than you. I am simply another soul doing the best I can. Like Jimmy, I want to grow, I want to heal, I want to be a kinder, more loving and more accountable person. I want to learn from my mistakes. And so, I dare to change.

Depression as Teacher, as Beloved Friend

What is this heavy, crushing sadness that sucks up all my energy, all my hope, that for no reason at all, appears at my doorstep, enters my home and leaves me limp and lifeless, wondering what plans I possibly had?

Depression has been a regular companion of mine for at least sixteen years. I have attempted to drown it in alcohol, suffocate it in drugs, silence it in denial, snuff it out with suicide, figure it out with therapy and fix it somehow. The thought of living with periodic depression, sometimes minor and sometimes so major that it takes chunks of time I can't even keep track of, for the rest of my life feels like a failure.

The linear narrative, the hierarchical structure, the capitalist dream, these stories we are told tell us that depression is a sickness, some bad and failed part of ourselves that needs to be out-run, out-thought, beaten into submission, overcome. These stories are hard to ignore. They seep in and saturate my consciousness telling me that I need to do better, telling me that my excessive sadness is a failure, that it is dangerous, that I must be doing something wrong if this is still happening.

But here is the thing, here is what I have learned, what my experience has been: there is no fix for depression, no magic word, no perfect solution, no cure. Depression is not a failure, not a sickness, not something to be feared and shamed and buried and killed. Depression, this deep, draining companion of mine, is a great teacher, a wise presence that has a lot to say if I will only stop trying to shut it up, if I will only stop screaming at it to go away.

When I have taken the time to be present with my depression, to go through it, to hear it and witness it, here are some of the things I have learned:

I am grieving right now, deeply, and I need to feel this. I am in a toxic situation and something needs to change. I am denying something that desperately needs to be given voice. I am tired, I need to rest. I am angry and that anger has been turned inwards. I am spiritually starved and hungering for a connection with my divine. I need to slow down. I am neglecting myself. I am refusing to dream my dreams. I've had enough. This relationship, addiction, habit, living situation is bad for me and is draining all my life force away. Something is wrong, you aren't listening, something is wrong! I want to travel, I want to write. I am afraid. I want to love myself. I need to see the water. I need to lie on the earth. I need to tell the truth. I need time to regenerate. It is time for something new.

Depression, when honoured, when cared for lovingly, is a magnificent teacher. I have found many things over the years which help me to better hear the depression's message for me. From therapy to poetry to rest to nature to silence to coffee dates with my friends. But whatever gives voice to the heavy, heaving sadness is what I need to do because my depression needs to speak. I won't silence it anymore.

All That's Left is Love

Gradual, organic and integral... Integrating. These realizations have been coming over me lately, these strange epiphanies. They are not cognitive creations, rather they are spiritual awakenings. Things are donning on me. A year and a half into sobriety and two years into trauma work, I finally have enough space between the pain for these new awakenings to happen. They are strange, ethereal, weighted, earthy, expansive, intangible and ultimately, indescribable.

Maybe you already know this, but I just learned. We are all doing the best we can. There are many of us who are incredibly lost and hurting and who are hurting others because that's all we know to do. There are those of us who have begun to heal and who are peeling off layer after layer of paint, all these thin layers of paint piled on top of each other that made the room so much smaller. Now we can breathe. There are windows we didn't even know about.

I am learning the difference between accountability and blame. I am learning the difference between remorse and shame. I am learning that good people do bad things. And I know that we were all little children once. I am coming to this wide open, expansive space in my heart where I can honour the goodness in all people while still protecting myself, honouring my truth and keeping myself safe. There is an endless compassion that I am realizing I have access to.

I forgive you. I know that you did your best and I know that you love me and I know that somewhere, somehow you are sorry and I am sorry too and I don't hate you anymore. All that's left is love.

Non-Local Phenomena

Where is my heart? I still ask that question but I have found that it has no location. It is diffuse. I have found that my poetry is recycled, cyclical, I have found that it spirals upwards forever and endlessly downwards, into the deep. I have asked you *where is my heart?* And you have answered me with eyes like questions, you have answered me, *how can what is infinite exist in any particular place?* I have found that I shine like an aching, pulsating star, I have found that all the shades of sky exist within me, I have found that hope drives me and that I am driven by hope. Yet I have not found my heart. I have not found out where it lies, deep in that chest of human flesh, I am escaping this. The sadness still comes. This longtime companion, this oldest of friends. Now I trust my sadness like I trust a map: I know that it is meant to lead me somewhere and I also know it is not entirely accurate, it is not the whole picture. I have memorized the bush in front of your house into which you threw a lit cigarette and I have learned never to ask what art *means.*

My meaning is meaning. I choose not to tell you what cannot possibly be told. Yet I feel all the feelings. I wrestle with my existential demons and I lie face first in the freezing cold snow. I surrender. I will not win this battle because there is no battle to win.

Desire / Power

I have been trained to be terrified of my own power. I play it down and avoid it. I don't want to be straight forward. I don't want to say what I like, what I want, what I desire. I don't want to tell you what to do. But sometimes the circumstances are conducive to granting me that permission. The look in his eyes, his arms up above his head, he is beautiful and my desire for him is more guiding than any desire to be a pretty, complacent, pliable thing.

I am. Here. I am here.

He breathes heavy. I kiss his neck because I want to. I bite his shoulder and I relish his response. I press my body into his and it feels so good. I am learning that sexuality can be communicative, loving, respectful, honest, authentic, unscripted and spacious. We are exploring an unfolding and in this unfolding my power feels invited, my humanness acknowledged, my desire important. I love to hold him in my arms.

Just to be Alive

I surrender my self-loathing. I give up on my fear. It is what is and it is only here. I am filled with a sweet sadness, a bittersweet grief, a lingering remembering, a letting go of a left over longing. Goodbye, goodbye to what I was, goodbye to who I loved, goodbye. I surrender to this process. I have no control over it. I love all of this, even in its impermanence, especially in its impermanence, even with all the bravery that love takes, even knowing that it is more than I could ever have dreamed, this life that I now have, with all its fullness, with all its hope, with all its love, with all its goodness, I know that I deserve it. I love this life with abandon, with a full and honest heart, with all my history inside of me no longer defining me like it did before, I love my mistakes and all the wrong turns because at the very least they brought me here. I want only to give back this love that I've been given, I want only to work from this place of gratitude, expanding it and multiplying it, I want only to say thank you for giving me this chance. I am so grateful, so humbled, so awed. Just to live. Just to be alive.

Thank You

I wish you love. I wish you joy. I wish you happiness, I wish you hope. I wish you healing. I wish you kindness. I wish you courage. I wish you wisdom. I wish you love, lots of it.

I am grateful for every single person who has crossed my path and for every lesson they have brought. I am humbled by this journey and by the love I have found on it. I am encouraged and inspired by each broken soul who dares to try again. I am so blessed, so full of love. Thank you for everything.

2014

All My Secrets

I first came across zines when I was thirteen years old. The internet was still in its early stages then. I was a closeted queer living in a small town struggling with intense feelings for my best friend and equally intense feelings that I should be ashamed of myself for this. Also, I was being sexually abused by my grandfather and my whole family was acting like this was completely normal. I was extremely depressed and unhappy. I felt utterly alone.

Zines exploded into my world. Their pages were messy, raw, honest, rambling, vulnerable, courageous. The zinesters were writing about the very things that I thought I was alone on. People were writing about sexual abuse and surviving incest. People were writing about being queer and being happy about it. I was still stuck in my small town and my abusive family life but I knew there was a world out there. Zines were possibility, secret rebellion, hope.

My first zine was called *glitterduck*. I wrote it when I was thirteen years old and besides cutting out a cute picture of a rubber duck for the back cover, the zine was about sexual abuse, a serious medical condition I had at the time, depression, queerness. I didn't know how to distribute it so it mostly didn't go anywhere but the sheer act of making it was powerful.

By fifteen I was making and widely distributing zines. At this point, I have been publishing zines for about twelve years. I recently tabled the Toronto Queer Zine Fair at which I debuted the newest issue of my zine, *seawitch*. The fair was an amazing, affirming experience bubbling over with queer zinester exuberance and I felt at home. I felt that the little baby closeted queer sad and depressed kid that I was had finally arrived *home*.

I did a couple readings from *seawitch* at the reading portion of the fair. At the end, an acquaintance approached me with tears in their eyes and thanked me for a piece I had read, saying that it meant so much to them. After the fair I got a Facebook message from another acquaintance who had traded zines with me at the fair. They thanked me for writing about both my genderqueer identity and my mental health experiences because they had never met anyone who had both intersecting experiences, like them.

This is why I write zines. Because so many times I have felt all alone and zines have burst through that isolation reminding me that I am human, that I am having human experiences, that I am not and never have been alone. And the fact that my zines can also do that for others is amazing. So often, we live our lives trying to act like we have it all together, trying to act cool and calm and collected, wondering how the hell everyone around us has their shit so together when inside we feel so many things. Zines, in my experience, are a way to be honest. Sometimes it's hard for me to say "Oh my god, I'm struggling, I'm so overwhelmed, I'm so scared, I want so much and I'm in so much pain and I'm hurting and I'm angry." But I can write that in a zine.

I don't need to wait for anyone to tell me that my writing is 'good enough' or that what I have to say is 'relevant'. I don't need anyone's permission to make a zine and neither do you. Zines are a wonderful way for marginalized and silenced people to create space for our stories, to risk being honest, to reach out and to begin to build community. Zines mean so much to me. They have been a transformative force in my life.

MadFemme: Memories of Femme Resilience

There was so much inside me. There was so much intensity, grief, rage. There was this pulsing and pushing, this fullness and emptying. I was alive and skirting death, trying to make meaning out of moments, keeping myself alive. Madness was a word I didn't know yet but I definitely thought I was going crazy. I was losing my grip on reality. PTSD was a diagnosis I didn't have yet so I didn't know what dissociation was. I just knew that I didn't feel real. I felt full and I felt bursting but I felt out of touch with reality. I needed to draw close. I needed to find what would bridge the gap between my tumultuous insides and the rest of the world. I tried a lot of things: aimless wandering, suicidal ideation, talking to myself, writing words on my skin, snapping an elastic band against my wrist, self-injury, writing, unstoppable crying, sitting down on the floors of my high school rocking back and forth and pulling on my hair. I was unstable but I was searching. I was trying to find a way to stay alive.

Some of the things that I tried were healthier than others. Writing and talking to myself and aimless wandering really did me no harm. Something else that I found in those days of uncontrollable emotion was femme. I didn't know the word femme yet. I just knew there was great comfort in dark purple or neon pink lipstick, there was great possibility in shimmering lavender and electric yellow fabrics. Dressing up for the day helped me to feel alive. The intensity of the colours I chose matched the intensity I felt inside and helped to manifest my truth in the world. Femme expression was both a tool of survival and a tool of resistance. It was self-care, self-expression and a way to cope with dissociation. I often felt like I was invisible in those days, like I was flickering in and out of existence. My femme attire was an anchor, making me visible and indisputably real. It was also, like the cuts on my arms, a scream. It was a voice that had been taken from me. It was a way to shout, to yell, to say fuck you and fuck off. It was a way to declare my body as my own and my existence relevant and important. Glitter and lipstick kept my hands busy. Metallic turquoise fabric was a shield. Fitting as many colours as I possibly could into one outfit was a reminder that I was alive. Like a garden, like the summertime, I was here and I was alive.

When I got out of the psych ward the first thing I wanted to do was buy hair-dye. Bright, neon, hair-dye. The colour didn't matter as much as the fact that it had to be loud, fluorescent, frivolous, ridiculous, over the top, too much. I had spent two weeks locked up in a place that understood colour as various shades of gray and beige. I had spent two weeks denied my own clothes, forced to wear track pants and oversized t-shirts. The only clothing of my own I was permitted to have were my socks. My socks were orange and pink and purple and green, covered with hearts and polka dots and stripes. I received comments from the staff that they were "extremely colourful." But colour was life, it was temperature, it was texture, it was abundance and vibrancy and hope. In the psych ward there was no hope. There were no mirrors to see myself with, no colours to contemplate, not even any windows to gaze out of. It was sterile, cold, dead. My socks were my only link to femme in there. They were a tiny splash of colour, a tiny reminder of possibility, a tiny rebellion.

I was put in there for being crazy. More specifically, for being of harm to myself. I had developed the habit of self-injury and half-hearted suicide attempts. I never went to my classes and I regularly had breakdowns at school. I had good reason to be upset. I was fifteen years old and still in regular contact with my grandfather who had sexually assaulted me when I was twelve. I had also recently come out of the closet in a small-town homophobic high school. I was experiencing abuse at home and harassment at school. I was being called a dyke every day. I had no words to talk about the sexual abuse happening in my family. No one was protecting me or telling me that what was happening to me was not okay. I was overwhelmed, unhappy and unable to keep pretending that everything was fine. The silence and denial and betrayal began to bubble up inside me, spilling over and spreading out into the world. I was trying to survive. I was finding ways to rebel, to resist, to insist on life. I was oscillating between despair and ferocious hope. I was acting strange and trying to find new ways.

In the psych ward they were not interested in my reasons for being sad and acting crazy. They informed me shortly after meeting me that I had a chemical imbalance and would need medication. The problem was located within me and my faulty wiring. There was nothing wrong with the world I was reacting to. There was no mention of homophobia or child abuse. They diagnosed me with depression and overlooked the PTSD. They wanted me to go to my classes, stop cutting myself, stop crying so much. They wanted me to stop acting strange and to behave. In the psych ward displays of emotion were not allowed. Communication with other patients was not allowed. We were expected to be as quiet and controlled as the sterile environment that surrounded us. Excessive crying or rule breaking would be met with a needle, sedating the offender. I learned that my emotions, the sacred signals within me that told me when something was wrong, were not allowed here. Like my colourful clothing, my colourful emotions were deemed bad. So, I acted good and played dead until they let me out. I knew that I could never survive in a gray world so I hid my true intentions and dreamt of hair-dye as I lay on the rubber mattress at night.

On the outside I made a solemn declaration to myself. No matter how fucked up I was, no matter how bad things were, I loved myself. I loved the drive inside of me that did not allow me to stay playing dead. I loved that I cried and freaked out and did drastic things because I knew, in my gut, that these were drastic circumstances. I didn't fully understand what was going on. I didn't know that I had PTSD and that was why I felt so unreal and disconnected from reality. But I knew that the lessons I was taught in the psych ward were toxic. I knew that colour and emotion were important. I knew that there had to be a way to want to live, to feel alive and keep my vibrancy. I dropped out of high school and my life took many winding turns. I moved to Toronto to find other queers and get away from my abusive family. It took me a long time to get the help that I needed. I learned something though, something I kept close to my heart through all the years that followed. I learned that, despite what I was being told, I was not the problem. I knew that I was in a fucked up situation and that my cutting and my suicide-attempts were ambulance sirens, smoke signals, flashing lights declaring an emergency. My emergency was not heard, was not attended to, so I plotted my escape and I escaped. I got my precious, wild, crazy, queerfemme self out of there. I dyed my hair neon pink.

All of this happened more than ten years ago. I am now a fully grown adult. I am still crazy and I am still femme. I have found the words to talk about my experiences. I have found counseling that is politicized and that acknowledges and addresses trauma. I have found the appropriate diagnoses of depression and complex PTSD. I have found queer and femme communities. I have found my power and my truth. Now, from this position of far more power and stability, I can look back over my experiences and reflect. I am interested in the relationship between femme and madness. I am intersected in how femme people are regularly regarded as being overly emotional, how we are not validated and taken seriously. I am interested in how both femme and madness are regarded as being too much, over the top, in need of control. I see many similarities in the ways that femme people and mad people are dismissed. Our modes of expression are seen as frivolous, ridiculous, excessive and irrational. Our truths are met with suspicion. Both mad people and femmes are seen as incapable of objective truth, as if objective truth were something desirable, or something that even exists in the first place. Mad people and femmes both break the rules, challenging masculine, linear and rigid cultural values. We create spaces of new possibilities.

As a mad femme, I am particularly interested in the ways that femme has been a healthy expression of my madness, the ways that femme has been a tool of survival and resistance. Looking back I see that I turned to self-injury and lipstick for similar reasons. Lipstick however did me no harm. I now understand my femmeness as a way of reclaiming ownership over my body, as a way to manage my depressive symptoms, as a way to break through dissociation and remember that I am real. I understand my femmeness as a way to visually represent intense emotions, as a way to express, talk back, play and explore. Femme is a powerful way to be in the world, a powerful way to stay connected with aliveness, a powerful way to insist on the importance of my existence and my life. I see now that the psych ward did not want me to become a healthy, happy madfemme. They wanted to flatten me out, drain my colour and turn me into a normal, productive, useful citizen. They had no interest in my health or well-being. Rather, they were interested in rendering me docile. My brightly coloured socks were a quiet rebellion. My dreams of hair-dye were femme dreams of freedom.

I write this in a sequined dress. My hair is bright purple. It has been more than ten years since they locked me up in that gray place where femme was forbidden. Yet after all these years I have only become more femme. At this point in my life I am almost two years sober, it has been many years since I last cut myself and I no longer want to die. At this point in my life I am a colourful, femme, queer, mad person who is deeply invested in my own wellness and happiness. When I have PTSD and depressive symptoms, which I still frequently do, I have a toolbox for coping and for keeping myself safe. That toolbox includes community support, counseling, spirituality, writing, art and grounding techniques. It also includes neon tights, hair-dye, cute dresses and glitter. I am proud of my femmeness and of my madness. I am proud of the ways they combine and interact. I am grateful for my own resilience, my own resistance and for the ways that femme has kept me alive.

Just Queer

From now on my sexual orientation is queer. Just queer.

(For a long time I held on to the word bisexual. Mainly because I saw the word getting a lot of hate and I felt attacked by that hate. Bisexuality has been a part of my shifting queer identity as has lesbianism/gayness. I still hold that bisexuality is a valid identity to have but I have come to realize that it feels like clothes that don't fit right on me anymore.)

Part of this shift has to do with the fact that my queerness has nothing to do with the genders of the people I'm attracted to (and maybe everything to do with it too). I am not only queer when I am with women. I am not only queer when I am with other queer people.

Queerness, queerosity, queer, to me, is inherently multiplistic, subversive and rich with possibility. It is not an identity category so much as a shape-shifting, curious, playful, fierce, protective, brave, daring, changing way of being. Queer is a verb. To queer. To fuck with. To render unintelligible. To render intelligible. To make meaning while simultaneously destroying any semblance of meaning.

I feel so queer in my bright pink dress. I feel so queer when I'm talking theory with my queer partner, when I lie on top of them and press my body into theirs and look into their eyes. I feel so queer when my assumptions are exploded and I am encouraged again to unlearn and to learn. I feel so queer when I am with my best friends, laughing and smiling and feeling the love. I feel so queer when I'm by myself, alone in my own power and wisdom and company. I feel so queer when I feel accepted for all of who I am, when I am not asked to sever a part of me, when no one bats an eye when strap-ons and bra sizes and lipstick and binders are all discussed easily and naturally in one conversation. I feel so queer when I am being hated on, when I am told to shave my fucking armpits or when I get stared at for my overflowing cleavage. I feel so queer when someone says to me "I feel different than I thought I was and I feel like I can talk to you about it." I feel so queer when I am humbled, undone, reinvented, changed.

I knew that I wasn't a heterosexual by the time I was ten. I came out as gay at age fourteen in a small town homophobic high school. I then adopted the term bisexual when I realized I was also attracted to men. I moved to Toronto at sixteen and discovered queer. Along the way I shifted between gay, lesbian, bisexual, bisexual lesbian and pansexual but queerness was always a welcoming umbrella that I felt could hold me whatever shifts took place. I also discovered my femmeness, queering femme along the way by mixing it with my masculinity. I came out as tomboy femme and that feels right and true right now. I also get a thrill from signifying masculinity. I also like to be a femme with a dick. My armpit hair does not signify masculinity. It signifies femme. I find the meanings that feel right for me and I allow them to grow and change and shift as they need to.

I surrender and surrendering feels so queer. I give up on trying to know everything, on trying to hold meaning still. I watch it mutate right before my eyes and I give up resisting that mutation. Instead I allow it to transform me.

Queer feels right and I welcome the change. <3

A Letter to My Kinda Sorta Maybe Mightbe Friends

Dear friends and sort of friends and almost friends and acquaintances,

I am afraid of you. I think yr really cool and I notice little things about you that make me want to get to know you more and sometimes when I talk about how sad I feel on Facebook you send me really sweet messages and comments that pull at my heartstrings and make me think we could *really* be friends, but the thing is, I'm really scared of you.

I want to be able to hang out with you. Maybe grab coffee and scribble poetry in our notebooks together. Or wander through a park on a day a bit warmer than today. I want to hang out and talk about stuff and maybe get a little closer and maybe even start to trust each other a little bit. I want to tell you that I'm feeling pretty overwhelmed with life, that I don't have all the answers, that I'm really interested in learning new stuff but so much of the time I am so overcome with fear and I have no energy. I want to ask you how you're doing and listen with an open, honest heart and not try to fix or solve anything, just listen and talk about it.

I want to point out the graffiti that I like and share stories with each other about our cats. I want to tell you about how I'm in love and I can't believe it and I want you to tell me all about the travels you have gone on and I'll try not to get too jealous.

I want to ask you questions and learn stuff from you. I want to cook you food but I'm pretty weird about food and sharing it with other people even though I like cooking for myself.

I want to talk about music and maybe even tell you some music that I like but I'm actually pretty private about that and really weird about it too but maybe if you want to we can play guitar together sometime. I hope you won't judge me for not being that good. I really love to play.

I want to let you in. I don't want to hold all these messy, scrambling, rambling, vulnerable, sweet and broken parts of me back. I want to let you in. I want to love you and let you love me in the way that friends do. Maybe we can ride bikes together or just talk about random things and laugh.

I actually long for this. I'm tired of being lonely. And even though I do have friends, it is so hard for me to bring you close and let you in. I am so scared of you.

I want to go slow and take time and honour the process and all that. But I want to do it for real. Like, take the risk and let you closer. I want to stop pretending that I'm all cool and calm and collected and I got my shit together because I don't. I'm a nervous wreck. I'm an introvert. I'm socially awkward as hell but get me talking one on one and off we go. I know we could hit it off.

I feel like there are so many people on the peripheries of my life. Some of you even dare to come close, casting glances my way, slipping love notes in between the cracks in my walls, being kind to me. I take it in but not too much, I don't get my hopes up, I don't let you really see me.

Because I am afraid. I am afraid that I'm really a mess. That the whole thing will be a mess. That if you really knew me you wouldn't like me. And if I really knew you I couldn't trust you. And in the end we'll just end up hurting each other because isn't that what friends do?

And life is so messy and so rocky and there are so many leaps of faith and so many risks and I've learned to just stay safe and scared and alone and secretly wishing we could be friends but never reaching out my hands.

So this is my confession. A first step in that direction. An intention. To start trying. To be friends.

XO with love, Clem

Polyfeelings

I am sitting at a table with a group of friends. Across the table is my partner, my best friend, the person I am so in love with. Next to me is a person he occasionally goes on dates with. She's smart and cool and pretty and kind. We're all laughing and talking and I am feeling my feelings.

It's weird. I have been socialized to see other women as threats. I have been socialized to compete with other women for male attention. I have been taught that love is a scarce commodity and to hold on to it tight. I have been taught that real love is possessive and that sexual and romantic feelings should be reserved for one person alone.

I would be lying if I said that these messages I have received have had no effect on me. I would be lying if I said that fear and jealousy were not present.

I am interested in staying with these uncomfortable feelings. I am interested in observing them, witnessing them and not immediately believing them as the one and only truth.

Despite my fear, worry and jealousy, there are some things that I know. I know that he loves me. I know that I love him. I know that he and I have both demonstrated that love in action and continue to do so. I know that we have talked about our feelings honestly and that we have discussed what we are each comfortable with.

I know that my feelings for other people in no way threaten or lessen my feelings for him. So therefore, it makes sense to me that his feelings for other people do not threaten or lessen his feelings for me.

I know that I want to be poly. I know that I want both of us to be able to freely choose to be with one another without having to repress or ignore other desires we may have. I know that I feel trapped in monogamous relationships and I end up resenting it. I know that even though this is sometimes difficult, it's what I want.

I know that she, this other date of his, is very sweet. She engages with me directly and we interact with each other. It feels good. It feels honest. It feels respectful.

I know that I trust him. It's the strangest feeling in the world. My heart is open.

I am so interested in what love can mean outside of the confines of possession. I am so interested in the possibilities of intimacy, vulnerability, honesty and community that this honestly communicated arrangement can bring.

On another day, I have just met up with my partner after a date with a woman I am seeing. I am lying in his bed and holding him in my arms. We are talking about our feelings, our fears. I am so in love with him. I am so awed by our willingness to see each other as full and complex people. I feel so loved.

Femme as Fuck

I adore femmes. I notice and value femme skills sets. I appreciate the diversity and vast difference in the ways femme is embodied. I honour femmes. I see the sacred in femme rituals. I see the power in femme mannerisms. I seek femme.

I do not feel that femme is a dress code. I do not believe that there are particular and exclusive ways to be femme. I do not agree with imposing hierarchies on femme.

I have always been femme and as soon as I heard the word femme I knew that it described me. My femme embodiment has shape-shifted and changed over the years but it has remained femme. On the rare occasion I like to dress up like a boy, even a slightly masculine boy. This does not diminish or take away from the fact that I am femme.

Once, when I was talking with a friend about my armpit hair and the fact that the majority of the men I've been sexual with have been really into it, my friend suggested that perhaps they were drawn to my underlying masculinity. This actually pissed me off. There is absolutely nothing masculine about my armpit hair. There never has been and there never will be. My armpit hair is and always has been an expression of femme. When I started growing armpit hair, I was eleven years old. At that time I was massively enamoured with my body, my new breasts, my new armpit hair, my stretch marks, my expansive sexuality, my long hair, the way I moved. All of this, together, was an embodiment of femme.

I don't subcribe to notions of 'high' and 'low' femme. My femme is not lower than anybody's. I don't wear heels. I rarely wear makeup. I get dirty, ride my bike, skateboard and spill my coffee. I am still femme as fuck.

Femme is not something that can be easily defined. It is a feeling, a way of being and if you are femme then you are femme. It's yours to claim. It's yours to decide. One of the things I love about being femme is my love for other femmes. I love the way that other femmes do femme and I love the way they do it differently. I am impressed with femmes who wear heals. I am awed by eyeliner skills. I notice the small details of femme ensembles. And none of it takes away from my own understanding of my own ways of being femme.

Femme love and femme solidarity.

Making My Bed

The lovely woman that I'm dating showed me this app to download on my phone. It's a way to establish habits by focusing on one habit and recording it for twenty-one days. The first new habit I have chosen is to make my bed every day. And I've been doing it. So far it's been thirteen days and I have made my bed every one of them. I'm actually really proud of myself.

The thing is though, this is a total secret. I haven't told anyone. The reason I haven't told anyone is because I'm ashamed. I'm ashamed of myself that something as simple as making my bed is difficult and unusual enough for me to feel proud of myself when I do it.

I've been using my phone to help me out lately. I've created reminders on it so that it will buzz and remind me to take my supplements, shower, eat breakfast, make my bed, pray and other things like that. It's been helping. I haven't been doing everything all the time but I'm getting better at taking care of these things. Again, it's embarrassing that I need to set a reminder on my phone to remind me to shower and eat breakfast.

I frequently wake up depressed. It's bad in the mornings. I wake up in a state of confusion and depression. My PTSD causes me to have serious memory problems. So I have a hard time remembering what day it is, what I'm supposed to do that day and what basic things need to happen in the morning and what order it would make the most sense to do them in. On top of the confusion, there's the low mood. I just feel sad and the negative thoughts are coming hard and it makes it difficult to figure out what to do so I don't do anything, I just go back to sleep. Or if I do manage to get out of bed, I am in a state of confusion and depression and I forget to do the most basic things.

The reminders and the habit phone app are helping. Instead of just lying there in sadness and confusion, I can look at my phone and have a very small, very concrete step to take. Instead of overwhelming myself by trying to figure out the whole day or the best order, I just have to follow the simple prompts. This helps a lot.

But I'm really embarrassed when my phone goes off. Once my partner saw one of the prompts and I felt horrible. I know that he is really sweet and supportive and he loves me and he's always there for me during my lows and I know that he would probably be really happy for me that I'm finding something that is working for me.

But I'm embarrassed and ashamed and I don't want anyone to know that I have such difficulty with these things. I'm twenty-seven years old and I feel like I should be establishing bigger, more important things in my life than the ability to make my bed every day.

This is internalized ableism. This is the repetitive messages that my trauma and my depression are all in my head, that I should be able to just snap out of it. Even though I've been diagnosed finally, even though I've done years of therapy, even though I am open and out about the fact that I have PTSD and depression, deep down inside I am ashamed of the symptoms, deep down inside I still believe that I should be able to just snap out of it.

Writing about this is a way to break the silence. It's a way for me to say, yeah, I've made my bed for thirteen days in a row and that's a big deal for me and I'm really proud of myself. It's a way for me to begin to believe that PTSD and depression should not be sources of shame. I want to extend to myself the same compassion I extend to others. And I want to give others the opportunity to extend compassion to me by being honest about what I'm going through.

Drinking the Glue that Holds Us Together

The vast majority of community events take place in a setting where alcohol is served. Even when they don't, such as a lecture for example, there are frequently comments made which draw attention to the normalcy of drinking. These comments are so common that they are ubiquitous. They go unnoticed in the natural, normal flow of things.

Recently, at an event where alcohol was being served, the speaker said "You can tell we're celebrating!" and gestured towards his glass of wine. Everyone laughed. The comment functioned as a glue, binding everyone together. We may be different, in various ways, but it is understood that drinking brings us together. It is understood that everyone in the room will relate to the correlation of celebration and alcohol consumption. At the time this comment was made, I was sitting with a group of friends. There were four of us and we were all sober addicts/alcoholics. We cannot relate to the lighthearted and normalizing statement that celebration obviously means drinking. We are othered. We are outside. We are not bonded together with this glue.

At another event, one that was held in a university classroom and at which there was no drinking, the speaker was explaining that there would be a question and answer period at the end of the event, but went on to say that more interesting conversation would probably happen later, once everyone headed to the nearby bar. Again, everyone laughed. Again, the glue of intoxication culture worked to bring people together across difference. Again, it was assumed that we all relate to and like the idea of free flowing conversation over drinks. Again, I was silent.

Politicizing and critically analyzing intoxication culture is about more than accommodating people who don't drink. Creating sober spaces, which rarely happens in the first place, should not be constructed as an act of charity for addicts/alcoholics. Drinking and not drinking are not two equally valid options from which we can freely choose. Intoxication culture is more than just the regular inclusion of drinking at events. It is the production of a standard of normalcy. This standard of normalcy, if we can live up to it, produces a position of power.

The regular comments which assume and imply that social drinking is a normal, desirable and expected behaviour consistently work to other people who can't or don't drink socially. Some of these people include: people who do not drink for religious reasons, people who have legal stipulations which require that they don't drink such as terms of bail or probation, addicts and alcoholics who practice abstinence, some addicts and alcoholics who practice harm reduction, addicts and alcoholics who are currently using but who cannot control the amount they use, people who choose to stay away from drinking due to a history of addiction/alcoholism in their families, people who have trauma related to alcohol consumption, people who don't drink due to medical reasons such as taking certain medications, people who are breast feeding or pregnant, people who do not drink for political reasons and people who do not enjoy drinking. All of us, and I'm sure others who I have not mentioned, are excluded and rendered other by intoxication culture.

When we reproduce intoxication culture we create divides in our communities. When we reproduce intoxication culture we hold up a standard of normalcy and desirability that many people die trying to live up to. When we reproduce intoxication culture we leave people out. Can we find another glue to hold us together? Can we find other things to relate to each other with beyond the assumption that we all can and do safely enjoy drinking? Can we begin to think critically about the things that we say, the events that we plan and the role that alcohol use plays in our communities?

It is not the responsibility of people who don't drink to do all of this thinking and organizing. We need people who can and do safely consume alcohol to do the work of deconstructing intoxication culture.

Intoxication Culture and Consent

I want to write about this but I stop before I get started. I have a hard time finding the right words. When I talk about this I am shut down almost immediately or the conversation is glossed over, given lip service but no serious thought.

I want to talk about the intersections of intoxication culture and consent (or lack of it). Most of the literature that exists on consent states that consent is "uncoerced, freely given, sober". On paper we generally agree that we can't assume a drunk or high person is truly consenting. In reality, most people get drunk/high and hook up.

Before I got sober I would regularly engage in sexual activity when I was drunk. The people I was engaging with were often also drunk but not always. At the time I adamantly insisted that I had the ability to consent when drunk and was totally offended at the suggestion that I could not.

As my alcoholism progressed my body stopped being able to process alcohol in the same way. Drinking the same amount as usual (or less) started to make me 'lose time'. I would come to naked in some random bed with some random guy. I knew that sex must have occurred but I had no memory of it, no idea if a condom was used. I was not consenting to that sex, even if it appeared like I was at the time.

When I bring this stuff up I have had people get really defensive and tell me I have 'no right to tell someone whether or not they can consent when they are drunk'. And that's true. It's up to each of us to decide for ourselves. The thing is, even if I think that I can freely consent when drunk, I have no way of knowing if the person I'm engaging with is truly consenting.

I have no way of knowing how drunk they are. I have no way of knowing how effected they are by one drink or two or six. I have no way of knowing how they will feel about what happened once they are sober. I have no way of knowing if they are truly consenting.

I look back at my drinking history and I now see that a lot of the sex I had was actually sexual violence. I was wasted. I was no in a frame of mind to freely give consent. I also don't know if all of my sexual partners were truly consenting, because many of them were drunk too.

Since getting sober I will not engage in sexual activity with someone who has been drinking or using. It's a firm boundary for me. I don't want to risk engaging in activity with someone only to realize the next day that the person feels they weren't able to give true consent. Consent is important to me and it's just not worth the risk.

I know a lot of people drink/use before engaging in sexual activity. I'm not trying to pass judgment. I've been there and I've done it too. What I'm trying to do is start dialogue. There is a wide gap between our public stance that consent equals soberly given consent and our actual activity. We need to start talking about this stuff.

What if we talked with our partners about the role intoxication plays in our sex lives? What if we talked and thought about the role intoxication plays in effecting our own and others ability to consent? What if we admitted that we can never actually know 'how drunk' someone is or how they personally are affected by a substance that they took? What if we started developing dating and sexual cultures that do not rely on intoxication?

How does intoxication play out in your sex life? Have you talked about sex and intoxication with your partners? Do you assume that a drunk person is truly consenting? What would you do if they later told you they weren't?

Can we let go of our defensiveness enough to have these conversations? Can we let go of the fear that we may have breached consent enough to consider that maybe we actually have? Are there ways to engage sexually while drunk/high that are still consensual? What would that look like?

I just want to be able to talk about this stuff so that's why I'm writing this. I hope we can start to have these conversations in our communities, with our friends, dates, partners and lovers, and with ourselves.

Just a Few

When I was three months sober my friend, who is not an alcoholic and who drinks, invited me to a show. They warned me there would be drinking at the show but I decided to go anyway. I wanted to prove to myself that I could still have fun and do things I want to do. When I got there, people were drinking. People weren't wasted or out of control but there was a steady flow of alcohol all around.

I don't think I can put into words the way I felt. Awful doesn't cut it. I felt apart, severed, an outsider looking in on something I could never truly be a part of. I felt different, fucked up, unable. I felt like a failure, like 'Why can't I just drink like these people drink? Why can't I just have a few and have a good time?' But I knew that I had never had 'just a few'. I have never been able to do that.

I left the show feeling awful. In a bad mood, resentful at the drinking culture all around me. Resentful at my alcoholism. Resentful at my sobriety and recovery. I thought 'If this is what sobriety is going to be like, do I even want it?' But I knew I didn't really have a choice. I knew that drinking, for me, would never be the way it was for those people at the show. I would never have a couple and have a good time.

Drinking for me has always and will always mean black outs, violence, sexual assaults, concussions, ambulances, cops, saying and doing awful things, regret, vomit, unprotected sex, shame, humiliation, trauma. I can't just have a few, no matter how much I wanted that. I am an addict. Once there is any amount of alcohol in my system, there is a switch that is flipped and any and all reason goes out the window. I drink when I know I shouldn't. I drink when I don't want to. I have lost the ability to choose whether or not to drink.

I am now two and a half years sober. I have a strong recovery program. I am now at a place in my life where I have zero desire to drink or use. I wouldn't trade the best days of my using and drinking for my worst days sober. I love my life today. I love the person that sobriety has allowed me to be.

Being around drinking doesn't feel the same as it did at three months. I no longer feel that dangerous longing to be a part of something I can never be a part of. I am no longer at a risk of relapse from being in a space where drinking or using is happening. That being said, I don't love being in those spaces. My PTSD symptoms are frequently triggered by the lack of boundaries people display when drunk. I find it hard to communicate and engage with people who are drunk. And being around a bunch of intoxicated people is just not my idea of a good time.

If I want to go to a show or event where there will be drinking I usually go with my partner or some other friends who are also sober and in recovery. Together we share solidarity and protect each other. Together we remind each other that we are not 'other' and 'apart', that we can have friends, community, fun and togetherness too. We share that knowingness that only addicts in recovery share and we watch out for each other.

I am able to function relatively well in the world of intoxication culture these days. I can be around it and not want to drink or use. I can be offered a drink or a joint and say no without the slightest hesitation or desire. I see my sobriety, as an addict in recovery, as a major privilege. I know that many of my friends and other addicts out there are not at the place that I am at today. I remain ever aware that just because being around drinking doesn't make me want to drink doesn't mean that it's the same for every addict trying to stay sober.

And that is why the prevalence of intoxication culture makes me angry. For some of us it is life or death. For some of us that feeling of 'Why can't I just be like them? Why can't I just have a few?' is the first step toward a relapse. We don't all have the privilege of making it back from a relapse. Many of us die in active addiction, trying to make it back to sobriety.

Sober spaces are necessary. We need to show addicts and alcoholics who are trying to stay sober that they are welcome in our communities. To me, a sober space is not a space where someone who shows up drunk or high is turned away. Rather, it is a space that is not centred on drinking. It's a space where the flow of alcohol is not what ties everything together. It is a space where people who are privileged in their ability to 'just have a few' don't, just for an evening here and there, to create intentional spaces that value the work of recovery that addicts who are trying to stay sober are doing. It's a space that has the power to save lives.

Not too long ago, after a 12 step meeting on a Friday night, a bunch of my queer and trans sober friends in recovery were all planning to go to a queer show. There's a bunch of us and we go to meetings together and support each other in our recoveries and go to events together as a sober crew. We range in sober time from about eight years to brand new. One of my friends was fresh back from a relapse and struggling to stay sober. I checked in about the show and realized that there was going to be drinking. We didn't know this because it was not advertised and because it wasn't happening in a bar. But, intoxication culture assumes drinking as the norm.

I talked to my friend about it and they did not feel safe being around drinking so fresh from a relapse. Of course, I wanted to go to the show, to be with queer community, to have fun. But more than that, I wanted to show my friend that they are not alone, that the fact that they couldn't be around drinking right then does not make them 'alone', 'apart', 'other'. My friend and I hung out and went to the park and swung on the swings. I'm grateful that I was able to be there for them but I am also pissed off that my queer community rarely considers the access needs of sober addicts in recovery.

This piece is dedicated to the friend I lost who never came back from a relapse because she died during it and to every single person who is struggling with addiction, whatever your path and your recovery goals. I love you all so fucking much. To my friends and community members who have the privilege of being normative drinkers, please help make our communities safer and more welcoming to addicts.

Change

I want queer spaces that are not centred on drinking. I want addicts trying to get sober to know they can still have a social life. I want the decriminalization of all drugs. I want harm reduction information and materials readily accessible to all who want them. I want normative drinking to be recognized for the privilege that it is. I want more conversation around the relationship between intoxication culture and sexual violence. I want more conversation around consent. I want an end to the shaming and stigmatization of addicts. I want an end to intoxication culture as the norm. I want us to be critical and aware of the role that intoxication plays in our communities. I want safer spaces to be more than just lip service. I want the inclusion of alcohol at events to be listed with access information. I want abstinence and harm reduction approaches to be able to come into conversation with one another. I want to imagine new ways of relating to each other, new ways to socialize, new ways to honour and respect out differences. I want change.

Witches, Justice, Integrity and Faith

I am a witch. I call myself an intuitive witch because my spirituality came to me naturally, on its own, in my childhood and because a lot of my relationship to spirituality and magic was developed with very little outside information. These days I am trying to learn more and to find out about the sacred histories and knowledge systems of pagan spiritualities.

For most of my life I have been a lone witch. As a child, when I was experiencing incestuous childhood sexual abuse, I felt very alone. My parents didn't protect me from my grandfather. In fact, my father encouraged my grandfather's abusive behaviour and my submission to it. I was scared and alone and overwhelmed. At the age of twelve I had serious medical issues (I developed a brain condition for no known reason) and for a while the doctors were very unsure what was going on. I came face to face with my own mortality at a very young age while simultaneously dealing with the trauma and betrayal of incest. It was too much to handle and I had no adult guiding me through, protecting me, and helping me. So, I turned to my spirituality. My connection with the divine is what got me through.

I would leave the house at night. I would leave the house where I was not safe and I would go out into the wilderness. The darkness and the large looming trees did not scare me. They were my solace and my protection. My bare feet on the earth. My arms wrapped tightly around the trunk of a wise old tree. I knew deep in my bones that I was not alone. I knew that there was something so much bigger than me, and infinitely smaller, something beyond what can be perceived with the ways I had been taught perception, something ancient, and I knew this something loved me and was protecting me. I faced the terror of abuse. I faced the unknown of death. I laid my body on the earth and I was held.

As I grew older, I carried this spirituality with me, though addiction/alcoholism eventually came between me and my faith, recovery brought me back. I began learning the histories of paganism, ancient knowledges and ways of being in the world, the witch hunts in Europe and the histories of violent suppression of these sacred knowledges. I am still learning and I still have so much to learn. I also know that it is difficult to find this information, buried as it is under hundreds of years of silencing and suppression and that some of it was burned up, smashed and no longer has any material existence. That does not mean that it can't be known again. I believe deeply that the divine seeks to lead us home.

I am grateful that these days I am hearing more and more talk of witches and paganism. More and more of us are becoming open about our beliefs and our searching and are seeking community with each other. I am grateful too that I am seeing a politicized spirituality developing. I am grateful that the questions are being asked: What does it mean for us to be witches on colonized land? What does it mean for 'new age' spiritualities to be picking and choosing sacred symbols and customs from various faiths and cultures? Where has colonialism and cultural appropriation intersected with our seeking of spirituality? How can we be witches responsibly and acknowledge both our histories/experiences of oppression and our histories/experiences as oppressors? These are deeply important and spiritual questions to be asking.

Spirituality for me is a seeking of integrity. It is a seeking of wholeness and being in the world from a place of wholeness. It is a knowing of our interconnectedness and an honouring of that. It is explicitly political because to be political means to be cognizant and critical of relationships of power. We can only be together if we respect each other, our differences and our histories. I seek to be humble enough to remain teachable. My spirituality is rooted in justice.

Blessed be.

Jealousy is a Teacher, If I Will Let it Be

Being polyamorous, and a survivor of sexual violence, and a human being living in a world that consistently defines love as monogamy, and a woman living in a world that consistently defines my worth as my ability to be (the most) desirable, is difficult. I have to be honest and say that it is difficult. Yet, in my bones, it is what I want. I want to love and desire freely. I want my love to love and desire freely. And so I write this to explore this thing called jealousy.

Jealousy has wound me up, spun me around, sent me hunting for someone to blame, sent me down into the deep. Jealousy, that most ugly of emotions, is confusing because I know, I really do like who I am. I surrender to jealousy as teacher, I writhe under the pressure, I feel uncomfortable but I do not escape my jealousy by denying it, avoiding it or by trying to control their desire. I let it all be what it is. And I discover some things.

I am jealous of her desirability, yes, but I am jealous also of their desire. My desire is caught, like a word in my throat, like a bird in a cage, like a shoelace in a bike chain, it's bad news. My desire is a mangled mess, a language unspoken for so long its pronunciation feels strange on my tongue. My desire is a dead thing, a rotting corpse, a caged animal, a lost cause. I am so out of touch with my desire. And yes, I am jealous of her for inciting desire in them, but more than that, I am jealous of their ability to desire.

I have not allowed myself to be free. I have not allowed myself to spill over and explore and be curious and act. I have been ashamed of my desire. I have punished and hidden my desire. I have been terrified of my desire. I have converted my desire into the tidy need to be desirable. An endless, never-quite-fulfilled occupation to make myself into the most lovable or fuckable thing. But deep down, below the surface, is my want, my want to want, my want to act, my want to desire.

I am writing this right now and I am not trying to make it make sense. I am following the twisting turns of emotions and letting it lead me. When I let go, when I open my heart and let the jealousy flood through me, I see that I am utterly whole on my own. I am afraid, yes. Afraid of being abandoned, of not being good enough, of being taken for granted and compared. I am resentful, yes, of every single person who seems to want, and lust and desire and crush so much more easily and freely than I do. I am resentful, yes, of every person whose introduction to sexuality was not child abuse. That is the truth.

I am afraid of not being seen, not being important, not measuring up. I am afraid of being left behind. I am afraid that what matters to me won't matter as much to you. I am afraid to own my own desire. I am afraid to admit what I want, to even know what I want. It touches on some deeply buried place of shame. As a child I learned that sex was inherently dangerous, invasive and out of control. And now, to desire feels dangerous, invasive and out of control.

I wish I could write this in a clear, chronological and organized way but I can't. I hope it makes sense. What I have learned is that I am whole. My fear is my own. My resentment is my own. My history is my own. My judgment is my own. My assumptions are my own. My jealousy is my own. My journey is my own. My desire is my own. What I have learned is that no other person holds the key to my happiness. No other person could ever love me enough to fix any of this. This is a journey I must take on my own.

I am laid bare by jealousy. I am brought face to face with my naked, shuddering, powerful humanity. I am brought face to face with my grief, my rage, my terror, my power and my desire. I let the clawing, twisting, aching happen. I watch my desire like a wolf with her leg in a trap. I watch her struggle and growl and eventually release herself. Injured, she limps off, but she is free.

Jealousy takes me to the place where I remember that despite my feminism and my queerness I am not exempt from a culture that treats women like objects. I have not escaped the social conditioning that my ultimate goal should be desirability. I have not walked away unaffected, unharmed. Jealousy renews my commitment to feminism, it reminds me why it is still necessary for me to actively unlearn my internalized sexism. It reminds me that I must actively resist taking part in the objectification of other women, that I must actively resist a culture which encourages me to compete with other women.

My jealousy is rooted in trauma, child abuse, sexism, internalized-sexism, queerphobia, internalized queerphobia and monogamy-centric scripts.

To witness them, my partner, desiring someone else is a spiritual experience, in the sense that it gives me a choice: grow or don't. I choose to grow. Jealousy is a teacher. And what a teacher. Just because I am uncomfortable, frightened, resentful, bitter and any other string of emotions does not mean that I do not want my partner to be with others. When I look closer I find that these twisting feelings mean other things.

They mean: I want to desire freely and act on my desire. I am attracted to women and I want to act on that without feeling like a creep. (This is my legacy of being victimized, of living in a culture that objectifies women and not wanting to be a part of that objectification.) I want to relate to other women without competitiveness. I want to feel human and not feel like a sexual object. I want to feel special and important and loved by my beloved. I want to feel safe. I want to feel whole. I want to feel secure. I want to honour and heal the wounds of my past. I want to be honest. I want to be heard. I want to be comforted and reassured.

These things that I want are all within my grasp. Jealousy can teach me what I really want and give me the courage to seek it, work on it, ask for it. Pretending that I don't feel jealousy, that I am better than that, that I am beyond that, is a refusal to take a gift that is being offered to me. Denying my jealousy is shutting out powerful lessons that have the power to heal me. Jealousy is a teacher, if I will let it be.

Three of Cups

The three of cups has been appearing in my readings. It holds a very special meaning for me right now.

The three of cups shows three people standing together and holding their cups in the air. It's a joyous and celebratory card. It's about community, about coming together and being together. Because it is a cups card, it's about the heart, emotions, vulnerability, honesty.

This card asks us to open our hearts to the people in our lives. It asks us to find people who we trust and to open our hearts with them. It asks us to risk vulnerability, to be honest, to share our feelings, to express our love.

This card is a reminder that healing and growth cannot be done only in isolation. It is a reminder that we need each other. It dares us to share the contents of our hearts with those we cherish and love, to take the leap of faith and be with each other.

This card is very important for me right now. PTSD, depression, trauma, social anxiety and many years of always being high and drunk have left me feeling very scared of people. In my recovery and sobriety I have learned to begin to trust. I have let some people close to me, usually those who are also in recovery.

The goddess, the universe, is telling me that it is time to step forward into community, to reach out, to dare to be honest and vulnerable, to let people see me. Together, to drink from our cups.

Numb

I hear about a woman being stabbed, a woman being shot. I hear about another violent attack, another misogynist rant. A constellation of explosions is set off inside my mind. I remember my back against his kitchen counter when he picked up the knife and held it at me. Later he said it was a joke. We had been dating three months. I remember waking up in a tent being felt up by a well-known community activist and pretending I was still asleep because I didn't know what to do. Pushing him off when he started trying to take off my pants. Never saying anything. I see him around protests and I don't say anything. I think about the barely legal porn I knew my dad was looking at when I was a kid. I think about my grandfather pushing his tongue in my mouth. I think about my ex-partner fucking me without a condom after I said I didn't want to have sex, him telling me how sexy I am when I'm all sad and submissive, tears streaming down my face. I think about traveling alone for the first time and the way I pushed the table up against the locked door, just in case. I think about the looks and the stares and the hey baby what's wrong why don't you smile. I think about the drug dealer who pulled my shirt down and the boyfriend who gave me an STI because wanting to use condoms meant I didn't trust him. I think about the show where I got beaten up and dragged down the stairs by my hair. I am moving out of my body but my mind and maybe my mouth recount the stories, the violence upon violence, the terror upon terror. I think about the hole in the drywall where my whole body went through. I think about his hands around my throat, his knee on my chest. I think being on the floor, him kicking me in the stomach. I think about the words you fucking stupid bitch do you know who you're fucking with you will be fucking sorry you fucking slut running your pussy all over town your life is going to be hell on earth. I feel defeated. The rage and humiliation and terror and grief and I feel that no one really believes me. I think about the girl who yelled at me on the street 'you fucking liar he didn't rape you' and the cops who told me to let it go, to move on because he's moved on but he's still messaging me three years later calling me a lying slut. I feel helpless, that's the truth. I'm exhausted. I'm fucking numb.

Power: A Remembering

I was born with all my natural, divinely given instincts in place. I was born to be curious, to honour my own needs, to communicate my own boundaries, to speak my own truth, to be brave, to be honest, to be playful and to engage with life. I was born with the right instinct to express it when something was wrong, to move away from danger, to be outraged by disrespect. I was born with the right instinct to ask for what I needed, to not question my own worthiness, to seek that which would fulfill me. I was born a child of the living universe, divine. These gifts, which are given to all of us, are meant to be nurtured, developed and refined. We are meant to be taught the skills necessary to make the most of these gifts. Instead, most of us are taught that our divinely given instincts are wrong. We are shamed, neglected and abused. We are taught that in order to survive we cannot be direct, we cannot honour our own truth, we cannot set our own boundaries, we cannot safely move freely in our own divine selves.

I am realizing for the first time in my life that my feelings of helplessness and unworthiness and fear are not innate. They are learned. I am realizing that I have been taught to abandon myself and to deny my own power. I have been carefully manipulated into betraying myself. Through neglect, childhood sexual abuse and a culture that taught me that my best chance at getting the love and protection I needed was a careful mixture of submission and manipulation. I was taught that my truth would be punished, my boundaries ignored, my curiosity dishonoured and my courage shamed. I was taught that the world was a dangerous place, that I was unable and unworthy of protecting myself, that the cost of love was my dignity, my power.

I want to talk about power. Not power over. Not the sick and terrifying power of abuse, dominance, oppression, exploitation. But power from within and power with. The divinely given innate power in every life form, in every being. That voice, that urge, that energy, however buried, however smashed, however silenced and shamed, that remains. That deep part of myself that knows, no matter how much I have been made to suffer, no matter how much I have been told it is my own fault, that really, none of it is my fault or my doing or my lot in life. None of it. The truth, deep down in my bones. The power that reminds me, somehow, an echo calling out, a strange recognition that reminds me I am a divine child of the universe, inherently and irrevocably worthy. That power, that right instinct, that knows what to do, who to trust, which way to turn, when to go, what to say. That deep, deep knowing. I could never lose it and it could never be killed. Despite all the trauma stacked upon trauma it is still here. It always was.

And yet I am out of practice. This power, this innate knowing, is my first language but it feels strange on my tongue. It was my first movement and yet I move clumsily and with much hesitation when I embody it now. I struggle with it. I doubt it. I push it away. Then it comes up all of a sudden, demanding to be seen and it is executed poorly, not with its inherent grace. It feels awkward and inconsistent and uncertain but it is, of its essence, a steady, consistent certainty. It knows. It knows what it knows and when it does not know, it knows that and it knows what to do to find out.

For the first time in a very long time I am catching glimpses of this ancient, inherent, wise and divine part of myself. Out of the corner of my eye I can catch the movement of a raccoon in the trees, an owl taking flight under the cover of darkness. I see the look in the eye of the hawk, that certain vision and I know. Part of me, maybe most of me, wants to run, quick and fast back to my place of helplessness, of victimization, of trauma on top of trauma, because it's what I know, it's what I think I deserve, it's what I have become accustomed to. To take the leap, to trust the voice, leaves me feeling terrified. What if I have to stand alone? What if no one believes me? What if everyone leaves me? What if no one protects me? What if I'm wrong? What if it's not such a big deal after all? These were the questions I was faced with in my childhood and besides literally running away to fend for myself in the forest or staying and becoming submissive and manipulative and dishonest and broken and small, I had no options. But now, as an adult, I have options. I have the ability to listen to my knowing and act on it.

If I have to stand alone I will stand alone until I find my pack. I do not need to hand over my dignity for scraps of company. If no one believes me it won't matter because it does not make the truth untrue. I have the capacity to honour my own truth without external validation. I have always had this capacity. It is innate. If everyone leaves me I will wander alone, safe in my own power, until I find my pack. I do not need the company of those who do not honour me. If no one protects me I will protect myself. I am not wrong and I know it. The doubt is coming from without, not from deep within. My truth is there, unflinching. I know what I know. It is a big deal. My life matters. My dignity matters. My boundaries matter. My feelings matter. I deserve safety, respect, kindness and love. Nothing less will do. I will not stay and endure anything less.

Coming back into my power, my power which has never left me, which has been here all along, will at first be as awkward and clumsy as any remembering. It will come back slowly, bit by bit, then all at once, then slowly. It will move from a flash of recognition, an impression, a scent, a sound, to full blown embodied knowing. I will remember who I am. Each time I have this encounter with my deep, divine, knowing power and I choose to act on it instead of replaying the script of helplessness, I take another step back into my own skin. Each time I hear the call and I choose to answer it I remember who I am. I do not need anyone's permission or protection in order to live in this world, safe in my own knowing. I was born worthy of this world. I was born, instincts in place to protect, sustain, nurture and love myself. I was born with the ability to sniff out a bad situation, to sense danger, to know when to go. I was born with the ability to seek love, to ask for what I need and want from a place of full worthiness, to find my pack, those I belong to. I was born a divine child of the living universe, deeply and irrevocably loved, worthy of this world, deserving of safety, love, respect, kindness. I was born with the power to protect and take care of myself. I have my own inner-knowing that can keep me safe and happy, that will lead me exactly where I need to go. I choose, right now, to listen.

Sober / Addict

I am a sober addict/alcoholic. I believe in the creation of sober spaces and the deconstruction of intoxication culture. I believe that, as communities, we need to look at the roles that substance use plays in our cultures and our lives. I believe that we need to be asking the question, when we include alcohol at (all) our events, who are we excluding?

We need to start looking at sober spaces through the lens of accessibility. We need to start looking at the ways that intoxication culture is complicit with rape culture. We need to look at the ways that intoxication culture is linked to ableism, gendered violence, colonialism, queerphobia and capitalism. We need to stop taking it for granted that drinking is neutral and normal and expected at every social gathering.

I feel like these conversations are starting to happen and I'm grateful for that. While we begin to critically analyze intoxication culture and politicize sobriety and sober spaces, it is important to remember that a critique of intoxication culture should not be constructed as a shaming of addicts/alcoholics. Politicizing sobriety should not mean moralizing sobriety.

A movement to deconstruct intoxication culture should centre the voices of those most marginalized by intoxication culture: the addicts and alcoholics. We have never been able to live up to the standards of normative consumption and we have always been pressured to do so. Whether we drink/use or are abstinent we are unable to have a normal relationship to substance use. We can't drink socially, as intoxication culture demands.

I am tired of seeing sober addicts/alcoholics, active addicts/alcoholics and addicts/alcoholics practicing harm reduction pitted against each other. I think this is a divide and conquer tactic. When we are infighting and criticizing each other for the ways we are trying to survive, we are not looking outward at intoxication culture. It is intoxication culture that created and insists upon a standard that we can't live up to.

For non-addicts/alcoholics who are sober, I have solidarity with you as another sober person. But know that my sobriety is not the same as yours. Know also that I have solidarity with addicts and alcoholics, all of them, using or not, practicing harm reduction or not, sober or not. Addicts and alcoholics are my people. A movement to end intoxication culture is not a movement to shame addicts/ alcoholics. Those are the voices that should be central in this discussion.

Heart So Full of Hope

For so long I lived in fear and despair. I kept the pain in my heart and wrapped around me like armour because it was all I knew.

I am just over two years sober. I am healing. I am working through trauma and PTSD. I have community and recovery and love.

I just got back from a trip to Montréal for the Montréal anarchist book fair. Walking through a park, it occurred to me that I was happy. Really happy.

I was alone for so long. I couldn't let the love in. I didn't know how. I am only just learning how.

I'm writing zines again. I'm working on a book of poetry. I have green hair and a heart so full of hope it scares the shit out of me sometimes.

I remember to be grateful. For all of this, thank you.

Crash and Burn

I feel like a total fucking disaster. My mental health has been incredibly unstable lately. I self-injured for the first time in years. I have been experiencing a lot of suicidal ideation, intense depression, nightmares, anxiety and dissociation. I have been living in fear. I have been isolating. I have been feeling so ashamed of myself.

I am over two years sober. I want to be better than this. I want to have moved on. I don't want to be depressed anymore. (I can remember being ten years old and crying my eyes out night after night, making sure to stop before I had to go to bed so that I wouldn't have puffy eyes in the morning for school. I have been unhappy for such a long time.) I don't want to have PTSD. I want to be able to go to shows with my friends without thinking about that time I was dragged down the stairs by my hair at a show. I want to feel a part of. I want close friends, intimacy. I feel outside, on the outskirts, unable to be honest and to truly connect.

Being in love with my best friend, being in a long-term committed relationship with someone I am head-over-heels for, is really fucking scary. I don't want to keep thinking about the abusive relationship I was in, the person who I thought was the love of my life who was not. I don't want to think about rape and violence and terror. I don't want to walk around on eggshells, enacting a trauma response. Because my partner is not like that. My partner loves me and treats me with care and respect.

I want to be able to trust, to have faith, to accept the many blessings in my life and to move forward, living in now. But fuck, I feel so fucking crazy. I spend so much time crying my eyes out. I am jealous and paranoid and having a really hard time doing the polyamory thing because I am so scared of being used and abandoned and taken for granted and forgotten.

I was trying to pretend that everything was okay. I was trying to pretend that my life was manageable. I was trying to pretend that I don't have PTSD. And then I couldn't pretend anymore. My depression and my PTSD and my alcoholism and my fear just overwhelmed me. I cried and cried and scraped my arm along a brick wall until I was bleeding. I hurled accusations and blame at my love. I isolated. I toyed with dangerous ideas.

I am finally being honest. I crashed and burned. I dropped the act. I admitted it. This is hard. I am really fucking traumatized. I am really fucking scared. I am so worried that truly, really, I am not loveable. I am so worried that this happy, healthy, sober life was never really meant for me. I am so scared that I really don't deserve any of this and that it will all just go as fast as it came.

I admitted these things and I cried and I showed my vulnerable, messy, immature, hurting side. I showed the worst of me and I am still loved. The world didn't end. I didn't do anything too drastic. I didn't drink. I don't need to relapse over it. I can be a mess and still be worthy of love.

I told the truth and I am still loved.

I don't have all the answers. I am not over everything that happened. Those things that happened will never not have happened.

Healing is cyclical. There are seasons to grief. I am still worthy of compassion and love. These are hard, messy lessons. Horrible, crying my eyes out and feeling like I'm going to die lessons. And I'm still okay, I'm still here, I'm still loved. I am exhausted and terrified and so grateful.

I don't know what's going to happen next. I don't know when I'm going to feel better. I don't know how to be happy right now. I don't know what the answers are.

Polyamory and PTSD

The truth is I'm so scared. I feel sick to my stomach. I'm having nightmares and anxiety and major depression.

The truth is I have never felt worthy of love. I am a survivor child abuse and intimate partner violence. It is so hard for me to trust.

The truth is that the fear and jealousy polyamory brings up for me is setting off my PTSD symptoms.

The truth is I don't know what to do.

Ethically I believe in polyamory. I know that my partner does not belong to me. I know that they have the right to have desires and experiences outside of me. Ideally it is what I want. It makes sense to me. But in my body and my emotions, I feel horrible.

Honesty is the foundation of my recovery and therefore the foundation of my life. So even though I am a mess right now and I feel totally lost and confused, I am trying to be honest.

My partner has agreed to put things on pause with their other dates right now. I am trying to figure out how to address my mental health.

I am trying to have compassion for myself as I work through this.

Gender-Nonconforming

I am a gender-nonconforming femme. I use the pronouns she/her. I have a vulva. I also sometimes have a cock. When my cock is being stroked and sucked, I feel it. It is a part of me. My large, heavy breasts and my hard cock are not a contradiction. They fit perfectly together.

A picture of me looking cute and femme in a tube top receives this comment: "I get the armpit hair. But do girls really have treasure trails?" The comment is in reference to the luscious line of hair that leads from my bellybutton to my pubic hair. Yes, girls can have treasure trails. Yes, femmes can have treasure trails. No, I'm not going to conform to your regulatory standards of gender. Yes, my treasure trail is sexy and looks cute beneath my tube top.

I like glitter and dirt. I like shoes I can run in and tights in bright colours. I like short-shorts and sitting with my legs spread. I put my arm around my partner when we ride the subway and I hold them in my arms when we sleep at night. I like to skateboard in femme outfits. I like to suck cock, eat pussy, have my cock sucked and have my pussy eaten. I like it when the fullness and fluidity of my gender is honoured and appreciated. I do not like it when perfectly natural and complimentary aspects of who I am are interpreted as contradictions or broken rules. I don't care about your rules.

My gender has always been fluid. I have experienced consequences for this, including physical violence. I have been assaulted in order to return me to a passive, appropriately gendered state. I have struggled to find the words to describe my experiences: my own experiences of my body, my gender, my pleasure and my experiences of others' attempts regulate my gender.

Right now, the word that feels right is gender-nonconforming. My gender has always been a rule breaker because the rules never made any sense.

A Note on Accessibility

If you are organizing an event and there is going to be drinking at the event can you please put that information on your fliers/posters and on the Facebook event page? Transparency about alcohol at events makes it easier for people to make decisions about which events they feel comfortable/safe going to. It also helps to start breaking down intoxication culture because it interrupts the invisible assumption that drinking is a taken-for-granted. We need more sober events. We also need the events that do include alcohol to be more transparent and accountable to our communities. I don't drink therefore I don't naturally remember and assume that drinking will be everywhere. I'm tired of changing my plans last minute because my communities do not accommodate or remember me and my friends.

Solidarity: People with Non-Normative Relationships to Substance Use Working Together

Recovery, sobriety, abstinence, harm reduction. These are loaded terms. They carry extreme emotional weight and value. The reasons we are sober. The reasons we use. The reasons we used to use. The way we approach recovery. The way we approach harm reduction. Whether we do twelve steps or not. Whether we are addicts. What our drugs of choice were/are. How our status as addicts/alcoholics intersect with our other experiences of power and oppression. How we take care of ourselves and each other. How we stay alive.

Building alliances with other people who have complicated / non-normative relationships to substance use, particularly those whose choices and experiences are different from my own, is hard, important work.

I know what saved my life. Twelve step work and complete abstinence are what I need to stay alive. This is my truth. For others, twelve step programs haven't been useful. For others, abstinence from some drugs and not others works. For some, harm reduction is what works.

I have to be honest and say that hearing about others' choices has been threatening for me. I have felt defensive. Primarily because I know that harm reduction, switching substances, cutting back and even abstinence without twelve step work, don't work for me. I know that when I tried to limit myself to a glass of wine with dinner, I drank the bottle, bought another, drank that and woke up in a park. When I use any drugs/alcohol at all I can't control how much I use and my life is dangerous. Harm reduction is not a choice that works for me. I need abstinence, complete sobriety.

At the same time, harm reduction saves lives. For many it has meant the difference between life and death. It is a strategy that works for a lot of people. Each person needs to decide for themselves what works for them. That choice should be freely made, non-coerced and supported. That choice should be made from a complete range of options. Addicts and alcoholics who practice harm reduction and/or are still in active use should not be shamed or excluded from our discussions about intoxication culture.

Whether we are sober addicts/alcoholics, people who use substances to manage pain, addicts/alcoholics who practice harm reduction, people who are sober for reasons unrelated to addiction, or whether we have any other non-normative relationship to substance use, we are all affected by intoxication culture and an expected standard of normative consumption. I truly believe that we can be allies to one another. We can learn from each other and support each other.

I am a sober addict/alcoholic who believes strongly in the critical analysis and deconstruction of intoxication culture. I believe strongly in the implementation of sober spaces in our communities. I also believe strongly in the decriminalization of all drugs and the wide accessibility of harm reduction materials and information. Solidarity with drug users. Solidarity with those in active addiction. Solidarity with those whose recovery is different than my own. Solidarity with people who are sober for reasons different than my own.

Thank you to every person who has non-normative relationships to substance use who has dared to speak your truth and tell your story. It's important.

Bodily Autonomy and Veganism

What follows is a short reflection on veganism. It is about me and my beliefs/experiences. It is not intended to shame or judge people who eat meat or dairy.

I became a vegetarian at the age of six. When I understood that meat was dead animals, I didn't want to eat it. My family and community ate meat but I was stubborn and stuck to my choices. My vegetarianism was met with hostility throughout my childhood both from other children and adults. A girl in my class rubbed chicken McNuggets all over my desk. I cried. When I told the teacher I was told that if I wanted my desk cleaned I would have to do it myself. I did. At camp I was served pasta with ground beef sauce even though the camp counselors had been told I was a vegetarian. I told them I couldn't eat it. They told me to pick out the meat. I threw my meal down the outhouse and didn't eat that night.

Looking back, I realize that many of the adults in my life were offended that a child felt the right to have such strong boundaries. I was insisting on my bodily autonomy. I was insisting that only I had the right to decide what would be going into my body. Looking back I realize that the family members who were most offended by and against my vegetarianism were the same ones who believed it was rude of me to object to the sexual advances of my grandfather. I was a child. I was supposed to do as I was told. I was not supposed to have ethical beliefs of my own. I was not supposed to have boundaries of my own.

Recently I have decided to go vegan again after many years of being a lacto-ovo vegetarian. I am reflecting a lot on my ethical beliefs and my history of vegetarianism and veganism. I am realizing that my belief in veganism stems from a core belief that the bodies of other beings cannot be mine. I cannot claim ownership over a cow or a chicken any more than anyone can claim ownership over me. I am realizing that my desire to respect the bodily autonomy of others was met with attempts to restrict my own bodily autonomy.

I am interested in exploring the links and interconnections between a culture of sexual violence and a culture of factory farming. I see a connection between a culture that promotes child abuse and does not respect a child's right to say no, and a culture that treats animals as objects with no consideration of their feelings or boundaries.

Gender\Queer

I stress about gender. I hate being called 'miss' or 'lady' or 'girl'. I hate being told I have to ride a step-through bike, also known as a 'ladies bike' or a 'girl's bike'. I hate being told that my body hair is masculine when to me it signifies femme. I stress about the fact that I know I'll never look like a boy, that I'll never be able to get my breasts flat enough and I don't know what to do with my long hair. So my queer femme masculinity is limited to pictures on Instagram. I hate that my nipples are considered inherently sexual and inherently pornographic and that it's a big deal if I take my shirt off. I hate the fact that my femme gender expressions are interpreted in a sexist, femmephobic culture of sexual violence as me 'asking for it', that my own gender expression is cited as the reason for the violence and harassment I experience. A guy told me that I have daddy issues, that I'm a hipster bitch in bright pink tights who doesn't know how to take a compliment, all because I asked him to stop interrupting my friend and I who were having dinner. My friend and I had to leave the restaurant because he wouldn't stop screaming at us.

I also revel in gender. I love being femme. I love being a gender nonconforming femme. I love signifying femme without wearing make up. I love femme as neon tights and running shoes, dresses that barely fit me, my breasts spilling out of them, going topless on a hot summer day. I love the tomboy femme struggle of bike grease staining really cute outfits. I love the complexities of my gender, the contradictions that are not contradictions to me. I love when my lover runs their fingers through my armpit hair or the hair on my stomach and knowing that my body is being held the way I know my own body. As femme. As genderqueer. As gender nonconforming. As genderfluid. As complex and human and me. I love it when I can pull off looking like a cute femme boy, rare as that may be. I love it when people tell me I look hot like that. I love femme solidarity, femmes standing up for each other, femme's complimenting each other's outfits. I love it when my silicone cock is treated like a part of my body, as real as the rest of me.

My pronouns are they/them or she/her. Coming out as genderqueer feels like a sigh of relief because it means I no longer have to section off aspects of who I am. I can be all of it. I struggled with coming out because being a woman is a part of who I am and I didn't want to give that up in exchange for space to be the parts of me that don't fit into the box marked 'woman'. I realized that being a woman is a part of my gender but nowhere near all of it. I realized that my gender, which I stress about and which I love, which I revel in and am punished for, which I can't describe and which I seek words to describe, is queer. It's very, very queer.

On Writing This

I write to sort out my feelings. I write to think through my thoughts. All of this is process. There is no finish line. Even when this zine is done and printed and in your hands it's not a finished product. It is always liminal, a passageway, a possibility, a moment in time.

Like many writers, like many people in general, I feel a strong urge to just hit backspace and delete it all. The way I wish I could find every copy of some of my old zines and burn them. The way that writing and especially printing makes this all seem so permanent, so final.

But it's not. I know that it's not.

I am twenty-seven years old. I am an addict/alcoholic who is 837 days sober as of writing this. I am worried about the bees. I have been struggling with intense emotional flashbacks lately and I only recently learned that is what they are called.

I am often overwhelmed with the amount of violence and trauma in the world. I am often overwhelmed with trying to find my place in all of it, trying to find how I can do better than I am in living a life committed to non-violence.

Spirituality and my connection with the divine are what get me through. Sometimes they are the only thing. My understanding of a power greater than myself, who I choose to call goddess or the universe, is what gets me through.

Writing helps me to calm down. Writing helps me to take the feelings, the fears, the hopes, the worries, the thoughts, the ideas and the imaginings and put them down on paper, outside of me.

May I always be humble enough to be wrong. May I always be humble enough to learn more.

Seawitch

Mermaid is siren with her twin tails sewn together
(Her legs forced shut)
Siren is Sheela Na Gig with her legs wide open
relishing and brandishing the power and pleasure
of her vulva
We dye our hair green, purple, blue
and say we have mermaid hair, we
wear teal lipstick and turquoise tights
We hear a calling from the deep
some memory half-forgotten
lingering like knowing
on our lips
The word is
seawitch

Bodies

How long am I going to carry this weight around? I can't find a way to put it down. I am shot through with this.

Bodies, female and fragmented, inciting a desire that has always been dead to me. Bodies, all those lips and eyes, inviting, inciting, your desire. I feel nothing. My numbness hides a panic. I am a thing. She is a thing. You like our style, our legs and arms, our cute outfits, crop tops, the way we do our hair. It all becomes a blur.

But do you like me more than her? Because if not then I have failed. I am caught up in a competition that I don't consent to. I don't know how to exit the race.

You will never know the price. The price is a spike, a hook. The price is to be motionless. I can be desired but I am desireless. I am a thing. Bodies. And it is shameful to have let them in, to have let them win, to have spread my legs and laid beneath them, to have wanted, in the cheapest way, to have won, to have been, if only for a moment, a desirable, fuckable thing.

Love was never on the table. Love was never a possibility, an option. I was the meat, I was the child, I was the squirming running, feeling his greasy stubble rubbing against my skin, terror and nothingness and knowing there was no other way.

Desire is never separate from power. There is no innocence, no way to claim we meant nothing by it. No way to say we simply want. When we look our eyes change what we look at.

C-PTSD and Emotional Flashbacks

I avoided a diagnosis for many years. My early experiences with psych wards were traumatic, particularly a two week stay in Youthdale lock-down psychiatric unit when I was fifteen. Even though I struggled with my mental health from my childhood onwards I did not trust psychiatry.

In my twenties I finally got into trauma counseling but I insisted on a non-psychiatric approach which my counselor agreed to. About a year ago I finally got a psychiatric assessment mainly because I was planning to apply for criminal injuries compensation and ODSP (disability).

My diagnosis was Complex-PTSD. I had long suspected I had PTSD: intrusive thoughts, nightmares, panic attacks in my sleep, hyper vigilance and dissociation were very familiar to me. But I had never heard of Complex-PTSD. The psychiatrist explained that it was the result of sustained, ongoing trauma.

It is only recently that I have begun to learn about the symptoms particular to C-PTSD. As I learn more and I see the ways that my C-PTSD operates I am realizing that a lot of what I just took to be normal or "who I am" is in fact symptomatic of C-PTSD.

Because my childhood trauma took place within the context on intimate relationships (my family) a lot of things that trigger C-PTSD symptoms are within my current relationships. Before, I understood that constantly worrying about seeing my abuser, thinking I saw him, thinking I saw his bike, etc, was hyper vigilance. But now I am beginning to see that my constant worry that my friends and loved ones are going to lie to me, manipulate me, disregard my feelings and abandon me is hyper vigilance too.

Because my basic needs weren't met, because affection was denied, because I was not protected and cared for, I learned to live in a constant state of fear. I'm always looking for the betrayal because as a child my parents betrayed me. They did not protect me. They allowed me to be abused.

I am learning about the concept of emotional flashbacks. I understood before that the intrusive and vivid thoughts of assaults were flashbacks. But I did not know that the intense emotional reactions I have to perceived threats to my relationships are emotional flashbacks. My emotional response is totally out of proportion with what is going on in the present. If I suspect a friend or loved one is lying to me or rejecting me I respond with the level of intense emotion I

felt as a child who was emotionally abandoned by my parents.
I don't trust. I am always on the lookout for the betrayal.

It's hard to explain the way I feel about learning these things. I have behaved and thought this way for so long that I don't know anything else. I never thought that my intense fear, my depression, my isolating and avoiding, my trying to control and manipulate, had anything to do with my childhood trauma. In fact, for most of my life I had internalized the messages of my abusers and believed that I was wrong for making "such a big deal out of it". I thought that I didn't have it "that bad".

It's overwhelming to learn this stuff but it is helpful too. At least now, when I start having an emotional flashback I can ask myself if the feelings I'm feeling are about the present or the past. It won't necessarily get me out of it. But it's a start.

Touch

I want to be touched but I recoil from touch.

I run my fingers across your arms, put my hands on your back. I long for you to touch me. I want you to touch me, not sexually, but affectionately. *(I will take what I can get.)*

I wish I could hug my friends, casually put my arm around their shoulders, or rest my head against them.

I come from a home where there was no physical affection, no touch. I come from a family where I learned that touch was rare or it was dangerous. I learned the language of terror, incest, unwanted, forced touch.

My body feels like a cage. I am trapped in here. My skin calls out like brightly lit neon signs *touch me please* but my body language says *stay the hell away.*

I am starving. I want to feel closeness. I am so lonely and I have been so lonely for so long.

Call Out Culture and Binaries of "Good" and "Bad"

I want to start this piece off by saying that this piece was difficult to write. These are thoughts that have been fluttering around in my head for awhile but I have found it hard to put them into words. This is my attempt at doing so. I still have a lot to learn and to think about regarding accountability, power, violence, justice and community. I am open to feedback and dialogue.

Oppression and violence are systemic and yet are frequently treated as individual. I hear things like "but I'm not racist" or "that's bullshit, I would never sexually assault anyone" or "I know him, he's not like that". We act shocked and appalled by the accusations of oppressive or violent behaviour as if racism or sexual violence were monstrous, distant, impossible to conceive of, instead of the very fabric of the world we live in.

Oppressive systems are just that: systems. As a white person I am implicated in and benefit from racism and white supremacy every day of my life. I have the privilege to not be aware of this. I have the privilege to disavow my own racism. Simply wanting to and working on unlearning racism does not exempt me from my role in white supremacy.

When racist behaviour is pointed out white people usually respond with a statement that they are not racist and did not intend for the racist act to be racist. Racism is constructed as an individual choice rather than a system. White people deny responsibility by citing good intentions. We can deny our racism by stating our intention to not be racist and thus refuse accountability.

We also live in a culture of sexual violence. Sexual violence is normalized. Consent is not something we are encouraged to learn. When someone is accused of sexual violence the response is usually a complete denial, as in "I would never do that". But really, in a culture where sexual violence is normal, isn't it more likely that a breach of consent did occur?

Maybe we don't want to think we would ever do something like that, maybe we are survivors ourselves, maybe we are oppressed ourselves, maybe we truly didn't think what we were doing was violent, any or all of that may (or may not) be true. The fact remains that we live in a culture where sexual violence is normalized and none of us have been exempt from that education.

The culture of "calling out" creates a binary of "good" and "bad". It creates a situation where people who have caused harm are shamed and cast out. Or, as is far more common, the person who has been harmed is silenced, ignored, accused of lying or exaggerating, and not supported, because everyone agrees that the accused "isn't really like that", isn't one of the "bad" ones. There is no middle ground.

We locate complex systems of oppression and violence within individual people as if being oppressive were a simple choice. As if you can decide to be oppressive and you can just as easily decide not to be. "Good" people will know what is oppressive and violent and will never take part in that behaviour. "Bad" people are oppressive and violent because they are "bad" people.

Since we don't want to be deemed "bad" and cast out (and since we don't want that for our friends either) we cling to "I didn't mean it that way", "he would never", "I don't believe they would do that", "she's just not that kind of person".

I know what it's like to watch my communities do nothing because they like the people who assaulted me and refuse to believe they are "bad". I am painted as lying, exaggerating, causing drama, etc. when all I want is to feel safe. Yet, I know that my rapist didn't rape me because he is a "bad" person. If only it were that simple.

The fact is, people who have committed violence, caused harm and/or behaved in oppressive ways are our friends, loved ones, family members, community members, even the person looking back in the mirror. They are not "monsters". They are people who have done harm, people who have enacted violence in a culture that normalizes, excuses, rewards and encourages violence.

I want to imagine another culture where accountability can happen, where we can learn from it when we have caused harm, where survivors are supported, where oppression is understood as systemic (if you are part of a group given power by a system of oppression at the expense of an oppressed group, you can't simply opt out of and deny that power), where the shame of having caused harm doesn't outweigh the desire to do better.

I can start from an admission that I have caused harm. I can start from an acknowledgment of the power I receive on a daily basis at the expense of oppressed people. I can do the work of listening, paying attention, respecting spaces that are not for me, learning when I make mistakes, stepping back and seeking humility. I can own the fact that my own experiences of violence do not exempt me from responsibility for being violent or contributing to violence.

We can start by talking about this stuff. We can start by having these difficult conversations. We can begin to replace "I would never" with "what do I need to work on? How do I learn from this? What needs to be done to support the person I have harmed?"

As communities we can replace "I don't believe they would do that" with "how can we offer support to the person being accused while prioritizing the needs and safety of the person who was harmed? How can we create communities of justice and accountability? How can we learn from this?"

I think the first step is to acknowledge that violence, harm and oppressive behaviour, while awful, are not unthinkable. They are common. They are normal. They are going on all around us all the time. We are all implicated in these systems in various ways, some of us more than others. Therefore, we don't need resort to shock and denial. Instead, we can ask what needs to be done now.

A Femme with No Make Up

I am femme. Being femme is such a central part of me. It is such a central part of my embodied experience in the world.

I am a femme who does not wear makeup. I want to be able to talk about this, about what it means and how it feels to be a femme without make up.

But most importantly, I want to be able to talk about this without it becoming a criticism of femmes who do wear makeup. I am not in competition with other femmes.

I fucking love femmes. I love the vast array of femme embodiments and femme skill sets. I love the makeup skills of femmes who wear makeup. They are real and impressive skills.

And at the same time, not all femmes wear makeup. You don't have to wear make up to be a femme.

I don't wear makeup because I am a rough and tumble low-maintenance femme. I need to feel good with the way that I look when I roll out of bed in the morning. I need to move through the world without worrying about smudging or reapplying.

Again, this is not a judgment against femmes who feel good in a full face of makeup. There is nothing wrong with that. There is power in that. It's just not for me.

I have psoriasis and rosacea, both of which make appearances on my face. I get acne. I have other skin issues that have caused me varying levels of insecurity. It is important to me that I find a way to make room within femme for me, all of me and all of this.

Being femme does not have to mean being free of "imperfections". Being femme means performing a fierce femininity in whatever way feels good to you.

I would not be more femme in a face full of makeup. I couldn't be more femme than I am right now. I believe strongly that there is no right or wrong way to be femme, no hierarchy of femme, just a lot of bad-ass femme babes doing femme in our own ways.

Depression Does Not Define Me

Inertia. Inability to make decisions. No sense of time, moments blurring into a river of hours, days, months. No anchor.

"What did you do this weekend?" I search my mind for the answer, trying to hide my panic as I come face to face with blankness. I have no idea. I have no idea how to answer such a basic question.

Depression results in shame. Shame deepens the depression. I am trying but sometimes my feet are slipping on the rocks, I am falling backwards.

There is hope. I ask the goddess to help me. I pray. I accept the way things are and I pray for guidance. I ask for help to take right action. I try to be kind to myself.

I seek a balance between acknowledging and validating the reality of my depression and not defining myself through it. I am more than this. This is a part of me, a part of my experience, but it is not all I am.

Feelings

These feelings are contradictory but they do not make each other untrue.
I begin to panic as I approach a feeling that I have felt. The feeling is mine.
But the other feeling begins to react. It wants to wipe the feeling out.
That feeling has been declared a threat.
I have a tendency to believe the urgency, to hold the most painful, pressing,
    urgent feelings as the most true.
But I have felt other things.
I have felt an expansive, relaxing feeling. I have felt laughter and curiosity and
    safety and pleasure. I have felt these things too.
I have felt what it feels like to let go, to trust, to encourage, to believe.
I have also felt panic, danger, terror, worry.
One doesn't make the other untrue.

Dreaming of a Future

I am at a place in my life where I am beginning to imagine a future for myself.
I am in the process of applying for grad school. This is a really scary process
for me because it means wanting something for myself and going after it. I am
in a relationship that is so meaningful to me and that has a future which we
talk about. Most importantly, I am still sober and I see a future for myself with
recovery and sobriety at the centre of my life.

Active addiction was a constant repetitive process of giving up on myself, of
throwing myself out the window. I couldn't believe in myself or invest in myself.
I had no future. Recovery means believing that I am worth saving, that there is
a point to staying alive, that I deserve happiness and safety and love. Recovery
means putting in the work to build a future for myself and to not give up on that
future.

Even after two years of sobriety, it's still scary. It's even more scary now because
it's so real. In the beginning it was more like, okay, I will give this thing a chance,
I can't lose more than I've already lost. But there was a part of me that didn't
know if it would work or if it would last. There was a big part of me that didn't
think I deserved it.

Now, I have this new life, this new way of being in the world. I am a different
person than I was. I am now beginning to identify with this new conception of
myself as the real thing and to let go of the mental image of myself as the drunk,
high, angry, bitter, self-hating person that I was for so many years.

I am beginning to imagine a future for myself, a future based on who I am today
and the choices I make today. A future based on my recovery, my spirituality, my
sense of ethics, my hopes, my dreams and my capacity for love. It's so scary to
really believe that this is possible but I move forward, with faith.

Demisexual Slut (???)

During the years of my active alcoholism, I had a lot of casual sex. I had a lot of hook ups, one night stands and fuck buddies. I really strongly identified as a slut, even though I also had complicated feelings about the word and I knew that in a lot of men's eyes it made me 'damaged goods'. As a survivor of incest and childhood sexual abuse, I figured I was damaged goods anyway, so what the hell, I might as well enjoy myself. I wrote a lot about these sexual encounters and my identity as a slut in my old zines but I didn't tell the whole story. I wanted to seem bad-ass and care free. I wanted to feel like I could 'use guys back' the way they were using me. I didn't write about the fact that there were many times when I would try to kiss the guy who was fucking me and he wouldn't because he 'doesn't kiss sluts' and I would freak out and start crying. And I didn't write about the fact that I would fuck those same guys again, because I just wanted attention, affection, human contact and I had no idea how to get it.

I have had sex with a lot of guys. I have no idea how many. I also don't remember a lot of it. I have had sex in black outs and only put together that I had sex from the fact that I'm naked in some guys bed. I have not remembered having sex only to be told about it later. Guys have tricked me into having sex with them by telling me that I already had and because I was so drunk all the time I had no idea and I believed them. Then they would all laugh about it and laugh about me. I tried to pretend that this was all very empowering and truly what I wanted but the truth of the matter is that I didn't believe anyone would love me and I thought that was the best I was going to get.

Even after I got sober and took a break from sex, I would still insist that I was a slut. The reason I felt that I had to proudly declare that I was a slut is because my abusive ex-partner who I dated near the end of my drinking used to use my sexual history against me. He would tell me that I was a disgusting slut and that no man would ever want to be with me if they knew the truth about me and that I was lucky to have him, regardless of the way he treated me. I believed him because deep down inside I hated myself and I was desperate for love. His abusive behaviour was terrifying but at least he was around, not like those guys who fucked me and left as soon as they were done. Even a fuck buddy I had for five years would treat me with so much disrespect, saying he was on his way and then not coming over till 5 am. My abuser was my partner and it was the closest thing to love I'd known at the time so I believed him.

Once that all went to hell, escalated into extreme violence and ended in stalking and criminal charges, I went back to sleeping around and pretending to be happy about it. I decided to be proud of being a slut as a way of telling my abusive ex to fuck off. I wanted to prove him wrong. I wanted to prove that being a slut was fun and made me happy and that I didn't need love and I didn't need him. But I was still so unhappy and I would get drunk and let random guys fuck me and then cry my eyes out because I missed my abuser so fucking much. The pain inside of me was so expansive, so endless. The random guys fucking me were momentary relief from the pain followed by still more pain, more emptiness, more loneliness, more shame.

There is definitely nothing wrong with casual sex or with genuinely enjoying it. I enjoyed some of the casual sex I had. (Worthy of mention is that when I was working I didn't drink before having sex and I was usually treated respectfully by my clients. The sex work I did was generally friendly and pleasurable.) But most of the casual sex I had, I now understand as sexual violence. I was too drunk to consent. A lot of the guys I was having sex with weren't even drunk and I was so drunk I was blacking out, slurring, falling over, puking on them even. I was treated with utter disrespect. I was treated like a thing rather than a person. I no longer want to talk about those experiences dishonestly. The truth of it is that it was violence and it was fucked and I was desperately unhappy.

Into my sobriety I still clung to the idea that those experiences were what I wanted and that being a slut is who I was. I stopped having sex though because I needed a break from it to focus on my recovery. After a year of sobriety and a bit of dating I began to wonder if I could enjoy the type of sex I used to have sober. I let a random guy pick me up at a public library and went back to a motel with him and we had sex. It was exactly the kind of experience I used to have, exactly the kind of experience I thought I was all about, and I felt nothing. I wasn't turned on. I let him fuck me. He came. We left. The end.

I began to realize that I am not into casual sex. I decided to put the past behind me and to name it as the cycle of trauma and repetitive sexual violence that it was. This left me to wonder what exactly I am into. I wasn't sure. I was getting frustrated with dating and having really mediocre and sometimes really traumatizing sex.

I ended up developing a major crush on my best friend. This terrified me because my friendship with them was so important to me and I didn't want to jeopardize it. But I had butterflies in my stomach and feelings of genuine attraction plus a deep love and affection for this person. I ended up blurting out my feelings and my friend said they felt the same but had also been nervous about jeopardizing the friendship. And so, we began a romantic relationship, slowly and with great care.

We are poly so the question of what I am into, outside of this relationship, is still on the table. I know I love the intimacy and sexuality I share with my partner but for a while I had no idea what I was looking for with other people. Seeing my partner date other people and develop sexual relationships with them smoothly and easily confused me even more. It wasn't easy like that for me and I didn't know why. With my history of casual sex I didn't understand why sexual attraction was so hard for me to develop.

Finally, somehow, I came across the term 'demisexual'. As a sexuality that is on the spectrum of asexuality, I would never have thought it could have anything to do with me. Being 'into sex' was such a big part of my identity for such a long time, how could I be on the spectrum of asexuality? But, as I have explained, my experiences with casual sex were frequently not truly consensual and were often rooted in trauma.

So, I began to look into this demisexual thing. Demisexual means half way between sexual and asexual. For demisexual people sexual attraction develops after getting to know someone and developing a connection with them. Looking over my sexual feelings since getting sober and from before I began to drink, I see that my crushes and attractions always developed once I knew something about a person's personality. It was never about the way they looked. I am not attracted to any particular style, body type or gender (though I do have a deep admiration and respect for other femmes). People *become* physically attractive to me once I am attracted to them as a person.

This is why, I am now realizing, dating and developing crushes has been confusing for me. I don't just meet a person a few times and develop a crush on them. I might think they are a good looking person, like their style, think they are cool and respect their ideas. But that special light of attraction won't shine on them until I get to know them better, then all of a sudden I'm like "whoa, this person is really attractive, how did I not notice this before?" And with dating, I feel that it is generally expected for people to move quickly, to kiss on the first date and to advance into sexual behaviour soon after. This always feels fake and forced to me. But to shift from platonic to romantic feelings (which is the way I am realizing I operate) is risky because there's a friendship already there that could become quite complicated or lost. I definitely don't think that we live in a culture which caters to demisexuality. But at least I am beginning to understand myself and what is going on with me.

I am wondering if I need to reject 'slut' all together or if it is a word that can take on new meaning for me. Is it even possible to be a demisexual slut? Instead of it being about having sex without emotional attachment (or even basic respect or true consent) like I imagined it before, could being a slut be about having a profound respect for the power of sex? Could being a slut mean being free to feel attraction toward multiple people but in my own time and on my own terms? Maybe it could be.

Right now I am describing my sexuality as queer, demisexual with femme4femme leanings. I am excited to give myself the space and the time to explore and develop my desires. I am grateful to be at a place where I can be honest about and let go of my past, making room for who I am today.

Grieving

Sometimes I burst into tears after I have an orgasm. Not because I am triggered or because the sex was traumatizing but because the sex was infused with love and I was able to let go and be present with that love. Afterwards the weight of all the sexual violence I have experienced comes crashing down on me and I am filled with unbelievable grief. I grieve for the person I was, for the child I was, for the helpless, scared, traumatized, drunk, drugged, unsure, coerced, rushed, threatened, assaulted, manipulated, lied to, raped, shamed, degraded and told it was all what I deserved and that I should be happy, person that I was.

Sometimes it's really annoying to me that a I burst into tears like that, especially after really hot sex, because I know it worries my partner and they wonder if they have done something wrong. I try to explain it or I can't say anything but they hold me and tell me it's okay.

I write about this stuff because I know I'm not alone. I write about this because there are so many of us who carry the legacy and trauma of sexual violence. I write about this because this is my human experience, my truth, and it is nothing to be ashamed of. I write about this because I know my tears, though sometimes inconvenient, are ultimately utterly healing. I am grieving. I am grieving and making space for the love that I deserve.

How to Support Survivors / How to Support Abusers

How to support survivors:
- believe what they are telling you
- ask what kind of support would be helpful
- offer whatever kind of support you are able to give
- back them if they are seeking accountability from their abuser

What not to do:
- don't ask for details about what happened
- don't play 'devil's advocate'
- don't pretend as if they never mentioned it and continue to treat the abuser as if nothing has changed

How to support abusers:
- show them that you think abuse is not acceptable
- encourage them to seek help
- let them know that the survivor's needs must be prioritized

What not to do:
- don't enable them by acting as if nothing has happened
- don't prioritize their needs over the survivor's
- don't support them in making spaces inaccessible for the survivor

Witch's Remembering

It's almost the fall equinox (Mabon) and, despite the cold weather of the last week, today it feels like summer. The light and the darkness are coming into balance and we are moving into the darkness, retreating back into the world below for another winter. We are going back to seed, back to rest, back to the dark space in time where we renew.

Today I was walking in the heat that I've already let go of and I passed a family of toadstools clustered in the grass. I know that toadstools are a sure sign of faeries. I stopped to admire them and then continued walking. A little way up the sidewalk I almost stepped on a cicada who was slowly making their way toward the grass. I stopped and waited for them to cross so that no one would step on them. As I continued on I passed one of those coniferous bushes with the bright red berries, one that had grown so large it was bending over from its own weight. I remember a woman I dated for awhile told me that those berries are edible but that there is a certain part of them which is poisonous enough to kill a horse. You have to know the right part.

These three experiences reminded me of the magic of the world and evoked in me a longing. Lately, I don't know for how long, I have been feeling spiritually disconnected. I have been praying at my altar and reading tarot but I haven't been lying on the earth, talking with the trees and making time for them, going to the water to be alone. I haven't been doing ritual or giving myself the uninterrupted time to really be with the energies of the living universe in all her endless manifestations.

I also wish I had others to work magic and share spirituality with. I have always been a lone witch. I have found two barriers to working with others. One is that many different things can be meant when one says 'witch'. I'm not a Wiccan or a 'new-ager'. I'm open to working with witches on different spiritual paths but there needs to be some overlap, some resonance. I can only work with witches who see a connection between the spiritual and the political and who are ethical in their spiritual practice, meaning that they don't engage in imperialist cultural appropriation. Secondly, magic is intimate. It would take a great deal of trust and vulnerability for me to share this aspect of myself with others.

But I am open to it, universe, I am open to it.

I was talking with my friend Sabrina who is also a witch. It is always refreshing and rejuvenating when I have the opportunity to talk with other witches. They were telling me about the energies and spirits that we work with as witches and that we often work with them as if they weren't existing within their current context. For example, we invoke water without acknowledging the pollution of the water. We invoke earth without thinking about landfill. We considered what it would mean to meet the energies where they are truly at, to hold them and to be with them as they are. We also made a link to trauma with this, the way we are able to or try to be with ourselves and our loved ones as we are, with our trauma. Can we be with the energies in this same way?

These conversations reawaken the spiritual within me and I realize I have been neglecting my spiritual life. Today the signs were there. The magic was calling out to me, asking me to remember, to be present, to reconnect.

Collisions with the Past

So I am trying to apply to grad school. I had to go to York campus, where I did my BA, to get a few things sorted out. It was so weird walking around that campus, followed by ghosts of the person I was then. I did my BA during my active alcoholism, during some of the most painful and fucked up years of my life. I lived such a strange double life. I would spend my time drinking in parks and alleyways, having black outs, getting assaulted, going from one fucked up dysfunctional relationship to another. And then I would jump on the subway and head up to York campus and go to class. It's amazing that I got my BA at all.

I remember the pull of school. I did it at first because I was tired of making eight dollars an hour working forty hours a week in a sex shop. I wanted to go into debt and have money and not work. But I remember when my brain started to get pulled in, when I started to engage, when I realized (remembered) that I'm actually really good at critical thinking, at writing, that I love ideas. I remember the flickers of beginning to care about something other than alcohol, drugs and sex. But the pull of my addiction was stronger.

My third year of university I had stopped the drinking but was still smoking weed. I was living with the partner who would go on to terrorize, rape, abuse and stalk me, who would suck up years of my life in court proceedings. I was desperately in love. I remember the contradictions of taking women and gender studies courses and then going home to a partner who was abusing me. In fact, they used that against me in the rape trial. The defense argued that since I was a women's studies major I should have been well aware that what he was doing was wrong (if he had actually done it) and I should have left and reported right away. But all that theory, while I loved it, I could not love the way that I loved him.

I just found out that my GPA is actually below the minimum requirement to apply to grad school. My heart shattered. I actually want this so bad now. I want to move forward with my life. I want to have hopes and dreams and ambitions. I don't want to be mired down in my past. My grades for my final two years of school read something like this: A A A A F A A A D. I am really good at school and when I applied myself even a little bit I did really well. Most of my professors were very understanding when I told them what was going on, when I explained that I missed the exam because I couldn't leave my house because my stalker/ex-partner was outside my house screaming threats at me, my sister, my cats. I was allowed to write the exam at another time. I was allowed to hand in assignments late as I dealt with the police, the trial.

But some professors weren't so understanding, didn't accept late assignments or care what else was going on in my life. If I had tried, I probably could have fought those grades at the time, but with everything else going on in my life, with buying court clothes and puking in the office of victim services and calling to see if he got bail to know if I had to start watching my back again and finding a brick on my front step and one on my balcony, I didn't have the energy.

It's been over three years since that relationship ended. I have been sober for over two years. I really want to move on with my life. I want to let go of the nine years of drugs and alcohol and trauma, the three years where my life was dominated by that relationship and its aftermath. I want to move on. But looking at that GPA makes me want to cry. My past is lying in front of me now, causing blockages and barriers to moving forward. I am still going to apply. I am going to try to explain and to contextualize those grades. But I don't know if it will matter.

Last night I dreamt of him for the first time in a long time. I had one of those horrible dreams where everything that happened, the abuse, the violence, the stalking, the police, the trials, where all of that did happen but somehow we were back together, we had forgiven each other. In the dream I felt so much love for him. It scared me so much that it woke me up. I looked at my partner sleeping next to me in bed and I reminded myself what year it is, who I am now, what my life is now.

That GPA makes me feel like a failure. It brings my self-image right back to what it used to be: a pathetic drunk slut going nowhere. Even though I try to have so much more compassion for myself than that, even though I try to remember that being an alcoholic and having C-PTSD and experiencing so much violence are not my fault, even though I do not judge others in active addiction or currently experiencing violence, even though I am sober and my life is different now, it is so hard not to internalize those messages. Even though I have come so far, I have shame about being unemployed and on disability, I have shame over how much C-PTSD and depression still impact my life, I have shame over my past and the degree to which it still affects my present.

I am trying to make peace with my past and to accept where I am in the present and to move toward my future however bumpy the road. I am trying to tell myself I will get to grad school, even if it means having to go back and redo courses. I am trying to tell myself that I have accomplished a lot and I have so much to be proud of. I am trying to tell myself that my past does not define me, the choices I make today define me. And yet, I really just want to cry my eyes out, for everything that happened, for the time lost, for all the pain and confusion, for not knowing how to get out of it for so many years.

The World

The world, card 21, the final of the major arcana cards, is about wholeness, integration, connection and moving outward from the self toward the rest of the universe. This card represents to me the fruits of recovery. It means letting go of fear and beginning to trust. It means letting go of selfishness and living in service. It means feeling connected, included, safe and loved.

This card asks us to seek wholeness within ourselves. To view with acceptance and care all of the different aspects of who we are. To integrate in order to have integrity. To bear witness. To let go of shame. To honour who we are, who we've been and who we are becoming. To see our fundamental worth.

This card represents the point when 'self' and 'self-interest' shift to include more than the singular person, when we begin to see that there is no separation between our own well-being and the well-being of our communities, of all fellow beings, of the world. This card means letting go of the illusion of separateness and awakening to the knowledge that our connectedness is the fundamental truth.

I meditate on this card. In times of fear and desperation, in times of worry and wanting to control, I remind myself of this card and its message. Fear makes us want to retreat into ourselves, to protect what is 'ours', to regard others with suspicion. That way of thinking, while providing a temporary sense of control, actually increases our fear by increasing our sense of separation and 'me against the world' thinking.

When we dare to soften, to expand our hearts to include every other being and the entirety of what is, we begin to move away from fear and into faith. We begin to see that we are of this world. Blessed be.

Courage

A lot of what I've been writing about is letting go of my past and beginning to imagine a new future. These have been themes that have been intensifying in my life as my sober time increases, as I look around at my life and I can't believe it's really mine.

Yesterday, just as I was pulling this zine together, I got a call from my sister. My abusive ex-partner, with another ex-boyfriend of mine, had showed up at her place (the place I used to live at too) wanting to see me or to find out where I live now. She obviously did not give them the information.

It has been more than two years since the last trial. More than three years since the end of the relationship and I am still living in fear of him. He still won't leave me alone.

After filing a police report and going over safety planning with my sister and mulling over all the possibilities of what this means I was so exhausted. I just wanted to go to sleep forever, to collapse. I am exhausted. I am tired of the adrenaline, the terror, I don't want to live like this anymore.

Courage is not the absence of fear. Courage is not going it alone. Courage is faith, integrity, self-worth, humility and willingness. I've got what it takes to do more than survive this. I refuse to be intimidated even when I am scared.

I choose life, my life, this life. I have the courage to stand by that choice.

Three Names

Clementine Morrigan is my name. Yes, my real name. No not the name my parents gave me or the even the name the government recognizes me as. But it is my real name, a name I chose for myself. A first name, Clementine, reminiscent of childhood days enacting plays based on the song 'oh my darling Clementine'. A last name, Morrigan, after the Morrighan, Celtic Goddess(es).

I do get asked if it's my real name and why I chose to change it. I don't really have an answer for those questions, except that a name is very personal, very intimate, and it has to feel right and it has to feel mine. Clementine Morrigan is right, is mine.

But recently, I have given myself two new names. Even I can see how this may seem ridiculous. I already gave myself my own name, why would I need two more? Because I do. Because I am multiplistic and changing and growing into new names without letting go of my current one. Because I am poly, many, not one.

Violet Seawitch is my name. A name to mark a certain part of myself which I find it hard to put words to. Violet for some distant relatives of mine on both sides of my blood family. Violet for that part of me who broke all the rules and got into so much trouble. Seawitch for this zine, for the water, for my witchiness and depth. Violet Seawitch is my slut side, my sex worker side, my exhibitionist side, my troublemaker side.

Jason Star is my name. A name to mark that part of me that is masculine and male. The part of me that prefers the pronouns he/him. A part of me I have buried and pushed down since I was a teenager because I didn't believe anyone would take me seriously as a guy. I'm too femme. My breasts are too large. I would never 'pass'. So best just to forget it.

But this year I came out as genderqueer/genderfluid/gender-nonconforming/nonbinary. And I finally made space for this part of myself. Happily, my friends and loved ones showed me support. The validation I received made me feel so good. I decided to name this part of me, to give myself a name for when I am in boymode. Jason, because it always was my favourite boy name. Star, to be really really gay.

Clementine Morrigan (they/them or she/her), Violet Seawitch (she/her or they/them) and Jason Star (he/him or they/them) are all me, all my names, all manifestations of the vastness of my being. And it feels good to know I can have as many names and pronouns as I need. I don't have to choose. I don't have to restrict myself.

Girl/Child

I was told over
and over again
as a child that I was
a girl
I wore girl
as dirt in my hair
frilly dresses
dripping ice cream
cones all over my face

I was a girl
told to be proud of it
a certain way of being
elusive and related
distantly to
women's rights
and menstruation
a future and a past
I did not understand

Yet girl, this source of
pride and defensiveness
I soon understood
meant legs pressed tight
together
looming nameless
danger
Somehow being a girl
made being abused
normal

I grew but did not
outgrow girl
At twentyeight
I am still called a girl
I wonder when I will
outgrow it, if I ever will
arrive at woman
which has a distasteful

sound, expired
relinquished
released from the danger
and allure of girl

But I am not a girl
never was a girl
that which girl covered
over was the word which
I was
denied
that word is child

I was a child
not a girl
not a word which is
used to describe
both a six and
a twentyeight year old
I was a child

I am not a child anymore

Readied to Let Go

I am being reborn, slowly. My insides like tangled vines, untangling themselves in search of sunlight. My heart like a cup thirsty for water, it's edges brimming, seeking overflow. I am being opened, all my fears like blades, that sickening spreading of adrenaline, that panic alert, being softened, sweetened by a stillness. My night dreams make no sense, no linearity, no logic. My day dreams like pebbles sinking into the abyss of dark water, promising depths. I am being reborn. My hands emptied, almost emptied, I am being readied to let go. And to fall that fall that makes my stomach leap, my heart in my throat, my ribcage wanting to close, keep me safe but my eyes are open and I am falling. Where I will end up, I don't yet know.

Re/Un/Dis/Cover

Healing is not linear. It is cyclical. We revisit the same trauma again and again with new insight each time. As long as we stay connected to our journey we are growing, even when it seems we have been plummeted to the bottom of another depression.

Recovery means going under, going deep down. But we don't go there alone and we don't stay there forever. We go in connection, with compassion, we go with healing salves and full hearts, we go with pen and paper to record and bear witness, we go with wisdom and humility. We go to forgive ourselves, to find ourselves, to remember ourselves, to free ourselves. We go for the children we were, for the pain we endured, for the harm that we caused, for the ways we got lost. To recover is to uncover, to discover, to remember.

What a journey this is. There are times when I thought I would die. But for 984 days I have been sober. For 984 days I have been present to my life and my feelings and my wounds and my wisdoms. No matter how hard this journey has been, how deep the depths, how steep the hills, I have remained faithful to that spark of hope that brought me here. It is worth it. It is all worth it.

Unfold

The universe is so clever and so wise. Sometimes I feel like I am just dragging my feet, like I am going nowhere but really the pieces are all falling into place. Happenstance and coincidence are most sacred blessings. I have learned to pay attention, to notice the messages. Sometimes disasters are exactly as they should be. Sometimes the meaning comes from the strangest of places. I try to remember this but I forget it. I become irritated that things are going the way they are, I forget that this is the way they must go. It is not that fate is written in stone. It is not that I have no free will and that I am simply floating down a river which only has one course. But neither am I the sole creator, the designer, the wise and knowing god/dess who sees from another angle. No. Rather, this is cooperative effort. When I am willing and humble I can see that I am a co-creator, but I am not in charge. The possibilities are endless but there are also particular lessons, particular blessings, particular meanings that need to unfold.

December 6th

I wish bill c36 was not happening. I wish a movement to end violence against women prioritized protecting sex workers. I wish a movement to end violence against women was a movement to decolonize, centring the voices and strategies of Indigenous women. I wish trans women seeking refuge from violence were not turned away from services. I wish drug users and street involved women were not seen as disposable and asking for it. I wish disabled women were not shut out of the majority of services due to inaccessibility and ableism. I wish the imposition of borders did not keep women trapped in unsafe situations. I wish our dialogue around violence against women would expand to include the experiences of non-binary people who are misgendered as women. I wish community accountability was a real thing. I wish the police and prisons were not held up as the answer.

Feminine&Masculine

I really enjoy the experience of exploring my masculine side. My friend gave me a hat and showed me how I can use it to hide my long hair. This is very exciting to me.

I posted some pictures of me in 'boy mode' online and I received all these compliments. I really love feeling seen and appreciated in my masculine presentation.

At the same time, it makes me really aware of the privilege masculine people have. As a femme 99% of the time, I very rarely get treated that way. I am used to being seen as frivolous and vain for taking selfies. I'm used to being pushed into a competition with other feminine spectrum folks that I never consented to.

I think that, because of sexism and toxic masculinity, masculine people who are even slightly feminist or respectful to feminine people, are treated like special gems. Even in queer spaces, we flock to masculine people, we hold them up, we long for their attention and praise.

I want to de-centre masculinity. What would it mean to value a feminine/femme gaze as much as a masculine one? What would it mean if masculine people were not held up as authorities? If feminine/femme people were not read as shallow, over-emotional, a dime a dozen?

I have also noticed that in my struggle to find my gender(s) it has been femme and feminine people who have reached out and supported me, who have encouraged me and cared for me. The care work that femme and feminine people do is usually taken for granted and ignored. What would it be like to name this work as work? To value it? To be grateful for it?

I'm still figuring out how to talk about this stuff. I still feel like I don't totally have the words. But I feel it. I have always felt it, known it. But I have never felt it from the masculine perspective before, and this only confirms my perceptions.

I love my masculine side but I refuse to be uncritical of our celebration of masculinity and the ways it takes up space in our communities.

Learning to be Loved

I'm a survivor of intimate partner violence. My ex expected me to be an endlessly sexually available porn star with no previous sexual history before him, a housewife who was always on top of cooking and cleaning, an around the clock submissive and a tomboy who could go just as hard as the boys and never complain. He wanted all of that wrapped up in one package which is actually impossible. If I fell short in any way, which of course I always did, he would berate me telling me how pathetic, ugly, slutty, used, worthless and not 'wife' material I was. He told me I was lucky to have him because no one else would want me and I believed him.

I am still unlearning this shit. I think I have to be perfect to deserve love. I think I have to be 100% what my partner thinks is cool, hot, sexy, whatever. I think that if my room is a mess I'm not worthy. I think that if my partner doesn't like a piece of clothing I shouldn't wear it. I think I have to bike as fast as my partner otherwise I'm not 'keeping up'. etc. It's fucked how totally embedded this way of thinking and acting is and how I just do it automatically.

Jealous/Panic

Self-loathing and jealousy. Comparison and never being enough. I sense strongly that these feelings are passageways to transformation if I can only approach them right. Yet I don't know how to approach them right.

I want to feel secure in my own skin. I want to trust that I am loved. I want to know that I am enough. Just as I am, I am enough. Just as I am, I am worthy of love.

I get this panic that comes over me. It is totally irrational but it is so strong. I compare myself to others and I worry that I fall short. This makes me feel anxious and depressed but more than that it sends me into panic because it makes me feel unsafe.

I am working on this stuff. It isn't easy. It's slow. But I am trying to see these feelings as keys to doors that need to be unlocked and opened. I am trying to see these feeling as signposts which indicate which parts of me are desperately in need of healing.

Dive Deep (Seawitch/Seagoat)

The winter solstice and the entrance into Capricorn fall on a new moon this year. A powerful space of darkness in which to let go, burn up, bury, heal, mourn, integrate, regenerate and then welcome the oncoming light. A little over a week later is my 28th birthday and the following day is the end of 2014. It's a time of endings and beginnings, a time of reflection, (re)collection, decision.

I am a Capricorn Sun and a Capricorn Moon. Capricorn is a seagoat. People often forget that and paint Capricorn as simply a goat. This does not do justice to the entirety of Capricorn's nature. Yes, Capricorn is a goat: methodical, stubborn, single-minded when its sights are set on something, hardworking, slow to change. But Capricorn is not just a regular goat but a seagoat: deep diving, spiritual, intense, reflective, passionate, with an eye for the mystical and other-worldly.

I am a Cancer Rising on the cusp of Leo. Big heart, compassionate and empathetic, maternal, nest-building, security seeking with a flair for the creative and the spotlight.

I'm Venus in Scorpio. Intense as hell, passionate, sexual, in touch with death and endings, with a tendency toward possessiveness.

I am lots of other things too.

I know I am a fish creature, a seagoat, a siren, a selkie, a seawitch. Morrigana. I know that the deep wide ocean, the bottom of lake, the seaweed is my home. Last night I dreamt about a lake, a very deep lake with very long tangles of seaweed coming up from the bottom. On the shore of the lake was a Virgin Mary statue. This is a real lake from my childhood and the message of the dream was to not be afraid of the depths.

So as this year falls into darkness and another year awaits its birth, I allow myself to dissolve into the depths, to dive deep, to let go of knowing, to be undone. May I be humbled, may I be open, may I let go of any resistance I still have to change. Blessed be.

Birthday/New Year

Today is my 28th birthday. Tomorrow is the last day of 2014. The end of the year is always especially reflective for me because my birthday is the day before new years.

Turning twenty-eight has filled me with that anxiety of getting older, that whole 'what the fuck am I doing with my life?' feeling. I am sometimes filled with a great deal of regret over the fact that I spent nine years of my life high/drunk/fucked up/hating myself/hating the world. I sometimes feel like I am so far behind and not where I should be at 28.

But I remind myself that the experiences I've had put me in a unique position to help others. I will be able to get through to other addicts/alcoholics/survivors in ways that others can't, because I speak from very real experience. I remind myself that this is my journey and I am exactly where I need to be.

I'm two years and eight months sober. Sometimes I feel like I haven't accomplished 'enough' in my recovery. In the past two years and eight months I haven't been in school, I haven't had any consistent work. And in the last year I haven't even accomplished too much artistically.

But I know I am being too hard on myself. First of all, my worth is not determined by my level of 'productivity'. I refuse to fall for that capitalist bullshit. Secondly, I have accomplished a lot. This is the sixth issue of *seawitch* I've written this year. I finished the edits on my book of poetry and I'm just feeling super shitty and anxious that the press is taking forever to get back to me. I have stayed sober. I have continued to do a lot of work in my recovery. I presented a paper at a conference in Minneapolis. I facilitated a couple workshops and did zine readings at a couple events. I got really good at tarot and did readings for people. I came out as genderqueer and started to really explore my gender identities. I applied to grad school programs.

I'm proud of myself even if it feels like I didn't do a lot this year. I had a pretty tough year mental health wise. That's the truth. I still feel a lot of shame over my C-PTSD and depression and the way they can suck up so much time and energy. But also, fuck that ableist bullshit.

New years and birthdays are times of reflection and also often times for setting goals. I find setting goals really hard. Like with everything else in my life I find it hard to find balance. I either make really lofty goals that are so far out of reach I don't even come close to achieving them. Or I'm really vague because I don't want to set a goal and not reach it, I don't want to admit what I want to do, I don't want to set myself up to fail.

Things I Need to Do to Maintain my Spiritual Health

- be with nature, stop to smell and touch and notice
- talk with the trees when they call, listen for their calls
- pay attention to the moon, pay attention to my body paying attention to the
    moon
- write poetry
- read and reread 'women who run with the wolves'
- light candles on my altar
- read tarot, meditate on the cards
- be grateful
- be humble
- ask for help
- accept what is
- pray frequently
- be of service to other beings
- don't worry, cultivate faith

2015

Three Lovely Things

1) I took a queer and trans specific ASL 101 class put on by ORAD (Ontario Rainbow Alliance of the Deaf). It was a great experience and I'm excited to sign up for 102 when I can. Learning a new language is very challenging and very rewarding.

2) I got a lovely new tattoo of forget me not flowers on my arm. The tattoo is by Alanna Mulé, the same person who did my raccoon tattoo. I'm really happy with it.

3) I am getting back to basics in my recovery. I'm looking for a new sponsor and I am going to go through the steps again. It feels amazing when I remember to make recovery the centre and foundation of my life.

Going Back to School

In *seawitch #5* I was freaking out about my GPA being below the minimum requirement for entrance into grad school and finding this out after I had made up my mind to go back to school. I was determined to try anyway and I did. I did a lot of work. Went into schools, talked to people, wrote and rewrote my letter, got people to look at it, wrote and rewrote my CV, got people to look at it, researched, stressed, changed my ideas, worried, kept at it and finally submitted 5 applications. Much to my surprise I have been accepted into 4 programs and waiting to hear back from the other one before I decide. So I am going back to school in the fall.

It's been a pretty shocking experience. My self-confidence has really been affected by my self-perception of myself as a traumatized alcoholic fuck up. I have so much compassion for other people but when it comes to myself I have internalized a lot of really harmful messages. I am almost three years sober (next month) and my life has changed drastically. I'm still not used to it. I still struggle with accepting that this is who I am today, this is my life today. I don't have to go back to where I was before. I get to move forward and keep growing and changing.

So, I am going to school in the fall. I have been out of school and any form of consistent work for three years. I have done lots of stuff but my life has been very unstructured. I am nervous but also excited to have some structure back in my life, to have goals and deadlines and classes. Most of all I am just really grateful that I got into school and that I have this chance. I am grateful to everyone who helped me and believed in me. And I am proud of myself for trying despite setbacks.

On Demisexuality

I recently came to the realization that I am demisexual. This means that I don't experience sexual attraction to people until I get to know them and for me, it also means that I don't have any desire to act on sexual attraction until a level of trust and familiarity has developed between us.

Learning this about myself was really confusing because for most of my adult life, which was spent in active addiction, I was hyper-sexual and struggled with compulsive sexuality. To get sober and discover that I am on the spectrum of asexuality was, and still is, really confusing.

I have had women accuse me of not being queer because I didn't move fast enough sexually. I have had people worry that I'm not into them because I didn't move fast enough sexually. I have spent so much time thinking slow down to the person I'm with or hurry up to myself because my experience of sexual arousal is slow, very slow. I can never seem to keep up. Most people lose interest and move on before I have even begun to feel or consider my desire.

All of this is wrapped up with trauma. I have C-PTSD and I am a survivor of a lot of sexual violence, starting in childhood. But just because my demisexuality is related to my trauma does not mean that it's bad or a problem or not real or not a part of me. Maybe I won't be this way forever and maybe I will. For now, it is my experience and it is valid.

I want to be honest about this because I am finding it really hard to find ways to communicate who I am and the ways that I feel. Many of the people I have been interested in since getting sober have not understood or made space for the way my sexuality manifests. I have felt like a failure, like I should be able to experience desire at the same speed as the people who want to date me.

I don't see examples reflecting back to me that this is valid way to experience sexuality. I only recently came across the word 'demisexuality' and recognized that there are other people who experience sexuality in a similar way to me. This was reassuring but I have still seen very little about it.

I want to find a way to bring demisexuality into conversations about sexuality, queerness, consent, communication, relationships, polyamory and desire. I want to see myself and others like me being included in these conversations. I want more complex and diverse representations of what sexuality can look like. I want to be respected, valued, included and understood.

Pregnancy Scare

Recently I had a pregnancy scare. My period is very regular and I always bleed with the same moon. I have sex that could result in pregnancy and I use condoms as my birth control. When my period was late, I started to panic, thinking that a condom had broken or slipped.

I am extremely pro-choice and for reproductive justice. I have counter-rallied anti-choicers and I've had the abortion conversation with many sexual partners. I believe fundamentally that the pregnant person is the only person with the right to decide whether or not to carry a pregnancy to term. I believe that abortion should be free, safe, accessible and without stigma. I also believe that support for child birth and pregnancy care should be free, safe, accessible and available to all who need it. Same goes for child care, health care and all of the things that would mean real 'choice'.

In Canada abortion is legal in most places but is also totally inaccessible in most places. Where I live, Toronto, I know that I would be able to access an abortion relatively easily. I am in a relationship with someone who would take me to and from the appointment, and respect my decision. My queer and feminist friends and community would also support me and there would be no stigma attached to me in the circles I frequent. This is not true for the majority of people who can get pregnant and I recognize that, in this, I have great privilege.

I mentioned to a friend that I was stressing because of a late period and they were just like "No, big deal. Abortions aren't too bad." They were trying to be supportive but in the comment was the implicit assumption that I would get an abortion. And in the circles I frequent, young, queer, broke, that is generally the assumption. The reason I was freaking was not because I was scared to get an abortion (which, by the way I am, pro-choice as I am to my bones, invasive medical procedures scare me in general) but because I was pretty damn sure I didn't want an abortion.

My partner and I have discussed having kids. It's something I would like in the not-too-distant future. Say maybe five or six years from now when I am making money and when I feel more ready and prepared to take on such a huge responsibility. But I do think I want kids. And I do think I want kids with this partner. And despite my belief in my right to have an abortion, it truly didn't feel like what I wanted.

Which is scary as fuck. I am not ready at all to have a kid. But part of my belief in reproductive justice is that all reproductive choices should be supported. I realized that if I wanted to have an abortion it would be easy, in my world, to have one. But if I wanted to have a child, it would be an almost unthinkable decision. Not only in the sense that it's not an ideal time in my life to have a child, but in the sense that I am not connected to any community where parents are common, included, welcome.

It got me thinking about how lopsided the reproductive justice work I've been a part of really is. Access to abortion is extremely important. So is access to having a child. I realized that if I wanted to do this my whole world would be turned upside-down. I had no idea where I would live. If I would be able to go back to school as planned. How I would financially survive. If I would be totally cast out of the communities I frequent. But I knew, in my gut and in my heart, that despite the unknown, I couldn't make myself have an abortion if I honestly didn't want one.

My period came. All the worry and projections of impossible to imagine futures vanished. But I was left with the lingering feeling that we need to do more to support and include parents and kids in our communities, that reproductive justice means more than access to abortion, that we should never assume what a pregnant person's choice should be.

Can Crazy People Be Poly? On Polyamory and Madness

My partner and I are polyamorous. We have been romantically and sexually involved with only each other for maybe seven months now. We started our romantic relationship poly because it's what we both wanted. We were both interested in dating multiple people. We both had some experience doing it, me more so than them.

I have been poly on and off since I was a teenager. Often it has been a wonderful and rewarding thing for me. Ethically and spiritually it makes sense to me. I love the idea of loving freely. I love the idea of relationships based on freely given consent and honest communication, free from a sense of possession or ownership.

I am also a survivor of child abuse, sexual violence and intimate partner violence. I have complex PTSD. Before this relationship my experiences with poly were mostly dating multiple people but without serious feelings. In this relationship I have serious feelings. Also, most of my past experiences with poly happened before the abusive relationship I was in, which seriously fucked up my mental health.

To my surprise, despite my belief in and desire for poly, I experienced extreme, terrifying jealousy and fear of abandonment. I told myself not to worry about it too much. I immersed myself in poly literature, zines, books, message boards, anything I could get my hands on. I read about and practiced observing my fear and jealousy, sitting with it, exploring it. I read about and practiced good communication skills, owning my own feelings without trying to control my partner's behaviour.

I believed I would get better at it as things got worse and worse. On top of my jealousy and fear was an intense feeling of shame. I was bad at poly. I was not doing it right. Despite all the work I was putting into it I was not able to sit with and observe my feelings. I was having panic attacks and thoughts of self injury and severe depression. Asking my partner to slow down on seeing other people felt wrong. Everything I read said that it was my responsibility to manage my own feelings without asking my partner not to do something they wanted to do.

I pretty much had a mental breakdown. I told my partner that I couldn't keep doing this. My partner was insistent that they wanted to do poly. I didn't think I could, as much as I wanted to be able to. I told them that my mental health was spiraling out of control. All my PTSD symptoms were extremely heightened:

nightmares, dissociation, intrusive thoughts, panic, hyper-vigilance, depression, anxiety. The beliefs I had internalized during my abusive relationship, that I have to be perfect to deserve love, that I am inherently unworthy and flawed, were dominating my thoughts constantly. I was afraid of hurting myself or even relapsing (I'm a sober addict/alcoholic). My feelings were so out of control. I hated myself for it. Yet I had to admit, finally, that this was the reality of how I was feeling.

My partner agreed to take a break from poly. We didn't specify a time frame for this break. They talked to the other people they were seeing and told them what was going on. Fortunately, they were understanding. We took a break from poly and I took the time to work on my mental health.

Now, seven or so months later, I have checked in with my partner a lot about my process and about their feelings about going back to poly. I never expected the break to be this long but I am grateful for it. My partner says it's no rush and that I can take my time. They also recently told me that they still need time to work on their own stuff regarding poly and communication. This no pressure break has given me the time I need to reflect. I'm still not the perfect picture of mental health but I am no longer having a mental breakdown.

Now that I'm not in crisis, I've become aware of something. Every single resource I have found regarding polyamory assumes as a given that the people involved do not have mental health issues. The advice to sit with and observe emotions may work for people who do not have mood and personality disorders, but for someone like myself who has C-PTSD, it's not that simple. My emotions include symptoms like panic, hyper-vigilance, severe depression, nightmares, suicidal ideation, dissociation and other things which are not so easy to manage.

At this point, I am hopeful that polyamory will once again be a part of my life. Yet I also don't know exactly how that will work or what it will look like. What I do know is that the current picture of polyamory is ableist and leaves no space for poly people with mental health issues. What I do know is that I'm not a failure, or selfish, for having C-PTSD. What I do know is that I'm worthy of love and that I deserve a partner and a community who are willing to make time and space for my particular mental health needs.

I long for resources and discussion on polyamory that include mental health issues. I want to talk about how polyamory intersects with trauma and madness. I want to talk about C-PTSD panic attacks and jealousy, hyper-vigilance and fear of abandonment, depression and your partner's other partners. I would like to imagine a polyamory that makes space for this, partners and metamours who make space for this, community that makes space for this. I want to imagine a polyamory that honours interdependence instead of the neoliberal idea that everyone is only responsible for themselves and their own feelings. I want to dismantle the idea that asking for what we need is shameful.

I also believe that by being honest about my own experience I may be able to start a dialogue. I invite conversation. I hope that we, as mad/crazy/survivor/ disabled people, can support each other, listen to each other, bear witness to each other, share advice and stories. I also hope that sane/normative people can begin to understand that mental illness is not a personal failing and that managing the feelings poly brings up is not a one-size-fits-all undertaking. I want to imagine a polyamory that mad / crazy / survivor / disabled people can be included in.

Spiritual Maintenance

Last night I lay in my bed and tears welled up in my eyes. I have been spiritually disconnected for too long. I have not been doing the things I need to be doing to maintain my recovery. I have remained sober but my heart and soul have suffered. I have allowed myself to engage in thoughts and behaviours that are bad for me and have neglected things I need to do for my spiritual health.

This morning I lit the candles on my altar and prayed. I drew cards and reflected on them. I took the time to really *connect* and I needed that so badly. I am already starting to feel better. I am remembering that I am not in charge, I don't run the show. I am remembering that living from a place of fear and control only hurts me. I can't afford to live like that. It is dangerous. I need to open my heart, let go, trust, surrender.

I know that the universe / god/dess / spirit / source / unknown is so much bigger and wiser than me. I know that I have been able to achieve and maintain my sobriety only through a connection to this divinity. And I am grateful. It feels good to remember humility, to remember gratitude, to remember that I am not alone and I am not in control. Blessed be.

TRAUMA TRAUMA TRAUMA

Some people talk about trauma and how it changes you and how you can never quite get back to the person you were before. But my trauma started in childhood, started in my formative years, while I was forming. So there is no before. There is no way for me to remember or access a part of myself that was well-adjusted, untraumatized.

The longer I am sober the more I realize how abnormal my 'normal' has been. I have been so fucked up for so long and in many ways, I still am. I am just more aware of it, more conscious of it.

I have never trusted people. Being a survivor childhood sexual abuse, not being protected by my parents, the emotional abandonment of that, has left me feeling like the world is dangerous, people can't be trusted, love does not guarantee a lack of severe betrayal.

My trauma made me fucking crazy and through my craziness I was traumatized so many more times. I have been assaulted sexually and physically more times and by more people than I can count. I can't even count it.

But I don't want to live in the cycle of trauma, being retraumatized, being fucked up and abusive to others, getting drunk and high and getting assaulted over and over again. I am so grateful that since getting sober my life has not been like that anymore.

But recovery is an ongoing process. The more work I do, the more I see how I'm still really fucked up. One thing that C-PTSD makes almost impossible for me is developing friendships and intimacies with people. I can't get close to people no matter how I try. I remain distant. I send off vibes of distance and therefore people don't try coming close.

Because from the perspective of my trauma intimacy terrifies me and makes me sick. I can never really explain it. Being an incest survivor is fucked. It confuses everything. It makes everything dangerous. There are no clear boundaries, no appropriate way of behaving. So it's best to just play it safe and avoid it all together.

But I don't want to live this way forever. I want to be close to people. I want to have friends, real friends. I want to be able to hug a friend in a genuine way, to sit together watching a show or just hang out together. It is really hard for me to do these normal things. Anyone who has tried to get closer to me will notice this strangeness about me. People praise me for my 'radical vulnerability' in my writing but in person I can barely say hello or ask you how you're doing.

I want to know sexuality in a healthy, clear, conscious way. I want to feel and possess my desire, something which is almost impossible for me. I want to know what I want, know what I like, trust that my desire is okay and not shameful and disgusting. (INCEST HAS FUCKED ME UP SO BAD.) I want to, maybe one day, have other lovers/dates and explore sexuality with others, especially with women, and not dissociate and not feel like a predator. I want to be cool with my partner being with others and not feel like I am being abandoned again.

Omfg trauma. Trauma, trauma, trauma. The story of my fucking life. But I want to grow, I want to heal, I want to wake up and be present to my life and try and trust people and I want to be loved and to love and to laugh and to have real friends. Maybe one day. Maybe maybe maybe. I hope so.

The Sacred Feminine (Gender Stuff)

Whenever I read something that is deeply, spiritually true for me, my eyes immediately and painfully well up with tears. This has always made the indifferent, detached space of academia difficult to navigate because I am *moved* by things. I feel them. Reading these words from Julia Serano's *Whipping Girl* on the subway today made me cry. "We must challenge all who assume that feminine vulnerability is a sign of weakness. For when we do open ourselves up, whether it be honestly communicating our thoughts and feelings or expressing our emotions, it is a daring act, one that takes more courage and inner strength than the alpha male facade of silence and stoicism."

My glasses got covered in tears as is so often a problem for me. These words were a fucking dagger to my heart because they are so true. Again and again I have been taught that femininity is a weakness. That my vulnerable heart is too messy, too much, an embarrassment next to the cold detachment of masculine posturing. Oh how I have longed to fulfill that posturing but even my masculinity is feminine. Reading these words resonated in my soul and reminded me that my ability to feel, deeply feel, to well up and over, to cry, to have heart, to be vulnerable, is and always has been a strength. Thank you Julia Serano.

Gender has been this whole thing for me lately. I am not taking my femmeness, my femininity for granted. I am exploring the ways that it has always been a choice, a deep desire made visible in strange colour combinations, glitter, hair-dye, tights, made visible in tears, voice filled with emotion, trusting the gut, the heart, and not just the mind. I see my femmeness, my femininity, entangled with my witchcraft. My intuition, my heart, my ritual, the way I am with nature, with the sky, the water, with my body, the animal that I am.

I am consciously and finally rejecting the imposition of a masculine Marxism that I was raised with, that denied me lip-gloss and nail polish, that taught me that these things were artifice and commodity, celebration of capitalism rather than adornment, symbolic, ritual, meaningful, like the way I light candles when I pray. The way this masculine Marxism passed down by my father tried to deny and hide the power of my mother who is and always has been a blatant femme. The way this masculine Marxism called my nail polish a commodity while obscuring the truth that I was the commodity, that I was not to adorn myself intentionally, express my sexuality intentionally because I was already owned. My sexuality, as survivor of childhood incestuous sexual abuse, was forbidden to me as something I could experience as *mine*.

And so as I unravel all of this and kick masculinity off its self-appointed pedestal, I am also in the process of discovering my own masculinity (and maleness) as a deeply buried, repressed part of myself. I am finding ways in which I can be a man, a guy, a masculine person and still also be a femme, a woman, a feminine person. And also unwrapping the ways that my inner masculinity was buried precisely because it is too feminine and I felt deep down that it would never be regarded as 'real'. I am letting all of my self, male and female and neither, masculine and feminine and neither, explore the divine space of sacred femininity. I am letting go of my shame.

More Will Be Revealed

Writing *seawitch* is a way for me to sort through my feelings, document them and watch my own process of growth and change. If other people get stuff out of this zine too, that's really great. I like perzines for that reason. They invite you into another person's world. For the space of the zine you get to see through their eyes and feel what they're feeling. And also learn from what they are learning.

It's Mercury Retrograde right now. Mercury Retrograde doesn't stress me out because I just slow right the fuck down. I'm grateful to be in Halifax at this time, working on projects, meeting cool people, walking around the city. In the mornings I've been doing my prayers and drawing daily tarot. There have been a ton of Major cards, suggesting intense things are brewing for me right now. Big changes that I am on the edge of, part of me is excited and ready. Part of me is really scared.

One of my favourite 12 step sayings is *More will be revealed.* When I am spiritually well I can trust that I don't have to figure it all out. If I listen for the guidance of the universe, if I take the right action to the best of my ability in the moment, things will be revealed to me. But the paradoxical, and I'm sure very common, truth is that I'm afraid to let go of fear. I'm so afraid to just trust and let go. My heart collapses at the first perception of a threat. My trauma brain is always on the lookout.

We've gone to the harbor here, but further south is a place called Point Pleasant which I want to go to before we leave. It's at the tip of the peninsula. I know that the presence of water has the capacity to heal me. I am ready to surrender to something so much bigger than me.

Gentrification and the Violence of White Guilt

We went to a community event here in Halifax about the gentrification of the North End. We learned a lot about the racism, segregation, classism and gentrification that is going on here. It was a good event in some ways and not in others. The main speaker was a white male professor followed by three Black women who were framed as 'respondents'. Then the floor was opened for community discussion which consisted of Black community members clearly stating what they needed white people to do in order to combat the racism in the community. And white people taking up space, talking about their feelings and saying they didn't know what to do. As a white colonizer and visitor staying in the North End, it gave me a lot to think about. It also made me think about Toronto and the gentrification and racist, classist, colonial violence happening there.

I recognize that white people need to shut up and listen way more than we do. Events about racism should not be centred around the voice of a white person. White guilt is just another form of white supremacy and racism. It is violent. When people of colour are expressing the pain of living under white supremacy it is racist and violent for us to talk about our feelings. We have a lot of work to do and it does not involve taking up space for talking about our feelings. I'm grateful that I got to go to this event and to learn more about the space that I am inhabiting while I am here. I also know that as another white person taking up space in this neighborhood, I am adding to the problem.

Some thoughts for white people to consider: What are we doing in our day to day lives to resist racism and white supremacy? Do we feel entitled to communities, spaces and cultures that are not ours? Do we recognize the violence of that entitlement? Are we willing to listen? Are we willing to act on what we hear? Do we include people of colour at our events in a tokenizing way or are we committed to centring the voices of people of colour? Do we consider the ways that all of our work and organizing is taking place within the context of colonization? What are we doing to centre Indigenous voices? Do we inappropriately bring up our own feelings when confronted with our racism? Can we begin to consider that forcing people of colour to deal with our feelings about our own racism is violent?

The Cuteness Matrix // Jealousy, Polyamory, Femininity

I've done a lot of thinking and praying and struggling and writing and reflecting and work on jealousy. I kind of just want to write jealousyjealousyjealousy all over everything, all over my face. I'm sick of pretending that I don't feel this or even that I'm some wise spiritual person who knows how to surrender to it and be transformed. Jealousy is one of my biggest issues. I've learned a lot from and about my jealousy but it still causes me a lot of pain.

Some context: my partner and I started our relationship poly but have been seeing only each other for almost a year. We closed our relationship because I was having a mental breakdown from my jealousy. I have had a lot of shame about this and feeling like a poly failure or whatever. But a lot of my soul searching since closing the relationship led me to realize and then write about the ways my jealousy intersected with my C-PTSD. I wrote an article about polyamory and madness and the lack of resources within poly communities for people with mental health issues. The article took off and I got a ton of positive ⟨ feedback. I realized I'm not alone and that jealousy, for people with mental health issues, is not always a simple matter.

Lately, another layer of my jealousy has become clear to me. This is about jealousy and misogyny. This is about my embodied experience as a femme (sometimes) woman who has been taught to believe that my worth and worthiness is tied directly to my desirability. This is about living in a culture that teaches me (and all of us) that feminine people are consumable and that we are in competition with each other.

I had this really amazing, healing, validating conversation recently with my friend Sabrina. We talked about the scarcity of decent dudes (for those of us who date/are into dudes/masculine folks), how there are so few guys who do not have serious issues with being misogynist and fucked up towards feminine people, and there is an overflowing abundance of cute, rad, babely, smart feminine people. And we, as feminine people, are expected to compete with each other for the attention of the few masc people who are decent. And then there's this pressure, that if we are less than perfect in any way, we can easily and readily be replaced. We called this phenomenon the 'cuteness matrix' in a half joking way. It was amazing to hear another person saying out loud the feelings I have had.

I don't feel like this phenomenon is specific only to those of us who are into masc people, but I feel like it's heightened there. Even those of us who have femme4femme leanings still live in a culture that imposes an objectifying and competitive climate onto feminine people. We are taught to regard each other with suspicion and fear, to perform our desirability the 'best', to have all the femme skills down from winged eyeliner to feminist politics to care work to acting like it all comes easily and naturally and we don't even notice that we're doing it. But we do notice that we're doing it and we do notice the femme skills of other femmes and instead of it just being a lovely and supportive femme4femme thing, it actually is far too often a stressful and terrifying thing about who is prettier and cuter and cooler and am I pretty, cute, cool enough?

I feel mildly embarrassed even writing these things. Because I feel like it's queer 101 that I should just love other femmes and never feel this level of insecurity and never buy into the masc-centric script that feminine people are in competition and easily replaceable and reducible to our ability to perform desirability. But the truth is that these messages are everywhere, they saturate the world around me, they are in porn and all over Tumblr and in queer spaces and on the street and on Instagram and at the local coffee shop and at the zine fair and everywhere. And I know that these messages have a lot to do with why I feel so jealous and I know that this culture causes me so much pain.

Another friend wrote me asking me about feelings of jealousy that are accompanied with anger and if I had any thoughts or advice on dealing with that. This is part of what I wrote in reply: "I find it helpful to note and validate the societal factors that contribute to my jealousy. Acknowledging that I live in a culture that pits me against other women / femmes, that defines my value through my desirability, helps to contextualize my anger. And honestly, this culture which treats women / femmes in this way is a reason to be angry. And it's not just like a personal thing to transcend and overcome but something that is beyond us that we deal with as best we can. I find that talking with my partner about this, once I have calmed down and done some work, helps. And especially I find it helpful to talk to other women / femmes who do poly and have a feminist analysis and can validate me and acknowledge the pain of living in such a culture."

The poly literature I have read does not address this shit at all. It does not address transmisogyny, racism, ableism and how these things affect the politics of desirability either. Mainstream poly lit just acts like we're all on the same playing field, that we have to 'own' our own feelings because they are ours alone. But actually, no. We are in community together. These power dynamics are not up to the individual to 'transcend' and get over. It is all of our responsibility to notice, name and uproot these oppressive dynamics. It's up to masc people to own their privilege and notice the way they interact with feminine people and make space for the pain feminine people feel living in this culture. It's on all of us to complicate jealousy and polyamory and to acknowledge the complex factors that make our experiences of these things different.

The Importance of Friendship

I move slow in general. I am a slow moving creature. It takes awhile for me to develop friendships. Coffee dates every now and again. Talking for an hour or two. These interactions add up and intimacy begins to develop.

Coming home from hanging out with a friend, I feel lit up, sustained. I feel like a plant freshly watered. I am realizing how important friendship is to my life. Even though I move really slowly, I need to make the effort to prioritize my friendships, to water and grow them.

Friendship is scary. The intimacy and vulnerability that develops with friends is so important, and really scary to me. Friend 'break ups' are so painful. And I feel like we are not allowed to really value and grieve friendships the way we are with romantic relationships.

I had a falling out with my best friend about a year and a half ago and it really broke my heart. We managed to make up to the extent that we are friendly to each other, but the friendship did not return. I feel like she really pushed me, she helped me to take those risks and get close to her. And I do miss her, a lot.

I have a couple close friends. I am starting to make a couple more. And I am realizing that this work is extremely important, extremely real and just as vulnerable and risky as developing romantic relationships.

To my friends, past and present: Thanks for everything.

Work and Desire: Reflections on My Experiences with Sex Work

What follows is some of my reflections on my experience with sex work. It should go without saying but I will say anyway that I do not speak for all sex workers, that my experience of sex work is not interchangeable with that of other workers, that my position as a white, colonizer/settler with access to university education puts me in a position of privilege compared to other sex workers and that one narrative about sex work can never cover the complexity and variation in experience of sex workers overall.

I used to be a sex worker. I was a broke university student living on OSAP. I was living with undiagnosed C-PTSD and depression that made holding down retails jobs hard. And, perhaps most importantly, I was an active addict/alcoholic who spent more money on my substances of choice than I did on rent or any other living expense. At the time, I was hyper-sexual. I hooked up with random men during my binges regularly. Since money was tight and I always needed more booze/drugs, sex work seemed like a realistic way to make money.

I was interested in porn but had no real way of accessing that industry where I was living. Webcam work proved to be unreliable, with the company taking a huge cut and the clients wasting my time. Stripping was probably out of the question because I was adamantly opposed to shaving any part of my body. So, I decided to give 'prostitution' a try. Through a conversation with an acquaintance, I learned that I could advertise on Craigslist (true at the time, not true anymore). So, I did. I created an ad, communicated my rates and limits and requested a picture of the prospective client.

My first attempt was an outcall. It was my worst experience. He told me to meet him at a corner and when I got there he showed up in a car which I had not expected. I got in and was driven out to a rich, fancy neighborhood which was unfamiliar to me. He insisted on smoking up first, wasting my time. When we got inside he gave me $160 when we had agreed on $200 and insisted it was all he had. He offered to throw in some weed to make up for it. Considering I had come all this way and was pretty much stuck out there, I decided to go through with it. I had sex with him and when it was done he drove me back to the corner.

From then on I did incalls. I was fortunate to be living with someone who was cool with it. The clients would arrive, pay 200 for the hour and we would talk, hang out and have sex. I never worked drunk even though I regularly went home with / brought home guys when I was utterly wasted, for fun. Work was different and I wanted to be alert. My experiences were overall extremely positive and pleasurable. Thanks to being able to advertise on Craigslist I was able to screen my clients fairly well. They generally turned out to be sweet and respectful. Except for that first experience, I never had a boundary broken.

During that time in my life I could not hold down a retail job because I would go to work way too visibly depressed. The eight hour or five hour shifts were torturous attempts to act like I was okay when I wasn't. Sex work was far more flexible. The 'shifts' were an hour long and I could schedule them when I felt up to it. The care work and performative sexuality that sex work entailed came naturally and easily to me. And I was paid far better than any of the retail jobs I had worked.

I ended up having to give up sex work because of severe, debilitating migraines which were, unfortunately, triggered by orgasm or sexual arousal. Later, when I decided to look into working again, I found that you could no longer advertise on Craigslist. I tried a few creative ways of meeting new clients but found it far more difficult to screen my clients and to state my rates and limits in clear, nonnegotiable ways. After a few attempts at working this way and some pretty bad experiences I gave it up.

At this point in my life I am almost three years sober. I am going back to school for a Masters program in the fall. I still live with and struggle with C-PTSD and depression. I don't work any kind of 'regular' job and live on disability. Overall, my life is extremely different. I no longer need to work to cover the massive expense of active addiction. I have recently come to understand my sexuality as demisexual. I have no desire for random hookups. I am in a long term relationship. And yet, lately, I have found myself desiring sex work.

This does not fit with the dominant narrative that sex work is something we do when we are troubled, that we move on from and grow out of when we are healthy. It also certainly does not seem to mesh with a demisexual identity.

The most violence that I have ever experienced in relation to being a sex worker was not from a client but from an abusive partner who I was with after I had stopped working. He knew about my past and would go into rages about it. He called me disgusting, a slut, a whore, etc. What infuriated him the most was my understanding of my experience of sex work as consensual, pleasurable, chosen, wanted. He could understand someone doing survival sex work because they had no other choice, but to want it was unforgivable.

I think it's very important in discussions of sex work to name and recognize the difference between survival sex work and chosen sex work (and the fact that the categories can and do overlap). I think it's important to recognize the privileges and choices (and lack thereof) that are available to us when we decide to work and to be aware that those privileges and choices are not the same for everyone. And I think it's important not to shame or pathologize any worker, regardless of why they work. Sex work is a valid way to survive. It is a valid choice of work. And the weight of those two sentences is different.

What would it mean for me to choose sex work at this point in my life? What does it mean for me to desire sex work? What about it do I desire? And how in the world does that work for me as a demisexual?

As a demisexual, I do not feel physically/sexually attracted to a person without getting to know them. But sex work, for me, was not about a physical/sexual attraction to my clients as much as it was a sexual attraction to the paid space of care work and sexual performativity. The intimacy I shared with clients, while real in its own way, was completely different than the kinds of sex I like to have with partners and lovers. It was contextual and without the context of payment and a mutually agreed exchange, I would not have been into it. If that makes sense.

At this point in my life I don't know if sex work is a real option for me. The increasing criminalization of sex work makes it very difficult to meet clients, screen them and work under conditions that feel safe and comfortable for me. Maybe porn will be in my future, since, for some bizarre reason it is not criminalized the way 'prostitution' is.

In the meantime, I just wanted to write this. Writing always helps me sort through my feelings.

Gender Ambivalence

I prefer it when people switch up my pronouns and don't use the same ones all the time. This is my way of attempting to deal with the ambivalence I have been feeling about gender.

I know people who *definitely* have a binary gender and then I know those who *definitely* don't. I feel lost in between that. I can't say with any sincerity *don't call me a woman, I am not a woman*. But at the same time, I don't really feel like a woman either.

Exploring my gender fluidity has been exciting and enjoyable but it is also painful and I also feel pretty lost. I just feel like there isn't language to express the way I feel about my gender. And also, that there isn't space for it.

I went for many years without bringing up these feeling about my gender and I could probably have continued. Because for me it isn't terrible being gendered as a woman. But it is getting more and more painful when I only receive 'she' without a question or a second thought.

At the same time I don't feel adamant about 'they' either. I'm not sure any of this totally expresses the way I feel about my gender.

As a kid when I had sexual fantasies, they were almost always heterosexual but usually there was nothing really straight about them. Because in my mind I was the man. I'm sure this had a lot to do with trying to make sense of my queer feelings in the context of the heterosexual matrix. At the same time I also feel like it was an expression of my genderqueer identity.

When I first got a strap-on I didn't even have a partner to use it with but I strapped it on alone and wore it around my apartment and fell asleep with it on. I have always felt that when I strap it on the dildo is my cock, not a dildo. And I feel really strongly about that. At the same time, I don't exactly feel male when I'm strapping it on either.

I remember being seventeen and attending a drag workshop and feeling intense pain at the fact that my breasts would not appear flat even with the binder. And leaving the workshops with fantasies of living my life dressed in male clothes and 'passing' while simultaneously knowing, under the fantasy, that I probably would never pass. And yet I love my breasts and I don't want to be a guy (all the time).

These days I'm just feeling pretty lost with it and that's where I'm at. If you want to be supportive, switching up my pronouns would help.

Not Alone In Jealousy: The Wisdom of Poly Failure

So I wrote "The Cuteness Matrix // Jealousy, Polyamory, Femininity" and then decided to post it on my blog. It blew up in a really intense way. It has received more hits than anything else on my website. I have received a huge amount of comments and messages and shares and the overwhelming response has been "Thank you for saying this! I feel the same way!"

It has been a really powerful, overwhelming and healing experience to see that I am really, really, really not alone in this experience. One of the most powerful parts of it was to see femmes who I have been particularly jealous of sharing it or commenting and saying they feel the exact same way. It kind of rips me open inside. It kind of floors me. It makes me feel entirely different about everything. It fills me with compassion and grief and wonder. I'm still letting the feelings settle. But wow. This whole jealousy and competition construct is pervasive and the femmes who seem (to me) to have it all together are suffering and struggling in the same way I am.

Another thing that synchronistically came together is that I am going to be facilitating a workshop on polyamory while here in Halifax. I went down to Venus Envy which is a sex shop/book store because the point person for the zine residency works there. While there I met some of their co-workers and one of them mentioned that they had seen some of my writing on polyamory and asked me if I would like to facilitate a workshop at the store.

So, I designed a little workshop called "Complicating Poly: Beyond Mainstream Narratives of Polyamory". Here's the description I wrote for the event:

"Mainstream literature on polyamory is generally devoid of political, intersectional analysis. The focus of most poly lit is the individual and the responsibility of the individual to manage their own feelings. There is no recognition of how things like jealousy, self-worth, communication and the ability to set boundaries are impacted by our social locations. There is no consideration of how power dynamics and oppressive systems affect our ability to 'do' poly and do it well.

This workshop aims to complicate poly by considering it along with gender, mental health and other social locations. It aims to offer reflections and considerations that will empower, support and lead us toward a more political, interdependent and just vision of polyamory."

There has been a lot of interest in the workshop online, including requests for me to do the workshop in Toronto, Ottawa and Montreal. We will see if that happens as organizing stuff is a lot of work. But it's exciting to see that these ideas are welcomed and that people want to talk about this stuff. It also feels really weird that people are turning to me and asking me to share my thoughts on poly because I have felt like such a poly failure.

But I guess it's time that we started talking about what it means to be a 'poly failure' and why so many of us feel like that and why so many of us are in so much pain and pretending that we are not. The universe really does work in mysterious ways and I feel like I am just on for the ride.

Some Things I Love

Traveling, writing, bike riding. Coffee dates, witchy things, hope. Possibility, magic, lighting candles. Resonance, compassion, solidarity. Bodies of water, tree roots pushing out of the earth, rainy days like today. Zines, plants, prayer. Tarot, remembering my dreams, synchronicity. Moments of realization, healing, growth. Good conversation, courage, femme brilliance. Cooking vegetables, collaborating on projects, hair dye. Sobriety, friendship, life.

Happiness

Happiness is this strange and striking beautiful thing. It actually makes me want to cry just thinking about it which is maybe paradoxical but – happiness is strange to me, new.

Today we went out to Point Pleasant and we were deep in the woods. Oh how I have missed the sanctuary of the forest. In Toronto I do not get enough of it but I grew up in the woods. I grew up in a tangle of branches, dirt all over my legs, the mix of light and shadow, the sounds of hidden movement, the life of the forest.

Being there today lit me up from the inside and I was happy.

I want to be happy. I just want to let go and to trust and to feel at peace. Trusting the goodness of my life, the possibility that I could be happy in an ongoing way, not all the time, but as a regular, normal thing, is heartbreaking, terrifying, seemingly too good to be true. And I want it, I want it so much.

Today I thought about it and I think I have been depressed for twenty years. I remember the time in my childhood when the deep, relentless sadness first hit, the terror and hypervigilance, the grief and the despair. And I had nowhere else to go except further down that path until the traumas added up and it was all I knew.

But now, my life is different.

And I think I'm almost ready to believe it. I'm almost ready to let go, to surrender, to be happy.

Remember When

Looking back at that first year of my sobriety, I was amazed by recovery and sobriety, blown away by it, but the world of active addiction was also painfully fresh. At the time of writing this I am just over three years sober. To say my life is different doesn't even begin to cover it.

The life that I have built today, the relationships I have, the work that I do, all of it is unbelievable if you knew where I started from. The friendly, kind and considerate person you see before you, who tries to continuously grow and change, is not the person with unfocused eyes, screaming and yelling, causing a scene. And yet, I need to remember that person. I need to hold her close. I can't forget where I come from.

I will never not be an addict. Even though I am sober and my life looks so different today, I am still a drunk. I don't say this to be hard on myself. I say it because I need to remember this. I need to remember that the life I have today is because of the work I do on recovery. If I were to pick up one drink I would be back where I started.

People find this hard to understand. People who have never seen me drunk can't imagine it. And the question is simple. Why don't use just have a couple? Why do you have to get so drunk? And the answer, too, is simple, but I think it's something that only other addicts/alcoholics truly understand. I can't stop. I am unable to. Something happens to me. Some subtle shift and change that makes all the reasons to 'just have a few' disappear completely and in their place is this unbelievable, unquenchable desire for more.

I have drank from an old beer bottle which was probably actually piss and we laughed and said 'Well hey, the person was probably drunk when he pissed in this bottle so there is probably some booze in it'. I have drank bottles of vanilla extract. I have gone through people's recycling bins looking for bottles that still had the 'moose piss' at the bottom and poured all that shit into one bottle. I have stolen drinks out of people hands, drank other people's cups left behind on tables, drank alcohol with cigarette butts floating in it.

When I was drinking there was always this underlying anxiety about how much alcohol there was. I was always eyeing the bottles, watching how much other people were drinking, worrying about last call or when the liquor store closed. That stress and anxiety was normal for me. I was that way from the first time I took a drink and literally didn't know that other people didn't feel the same. The idea of leaving an unfinished drink on the table and walking away is literally unthinkable to me.

It was only when I came into recovery that I learned this kind of thinking is typical for alcoholics. One is too many. A thousand isn't enough. So, no, I can't be a social drinker. I can be an out of control, extremely wasted, puking for days, getting sent off in ambulances person or I can be a sober person. There is no middle ground for me.

Remembering this helps me to stay sober and to keep building this beautiful life instead of tearing it to the ground. It also reminds me to have compassion for alcoholics, addicts, drunks, drug users and all the people society looks down on and shames. I am one of those people. Whatever I may look like right now, I will forever be one of those people.

Intoxication culture demands that people take the drink and leave the drink. I fail on both ends because I can't take it and I can't leave it. Intoxication culture is what pushed me to keep trying to be a social drinker even though I had proved to myself over and over again that it was futile. Intoxication culture doesn't celebrate addicts and alcoholics. It celebrates normative drinkers.

Addicts and alcoholics, wherever you are on your journey, if you are in active use, want to stop, never want to stop, practice harm reduction, practice 12 steps, are sober, are struggling, I fucking love you from the bottom of my heart.

Sobriety Is An Energy

I've been thinking about sobriety as an energy lately. Sobriety is usually thought of an absence, a lack; it is defined by what it is not. You are sober if you not intoxicated. Sobriety is the absence of intoxication. But I can say that my experience of three consecutive years of complete sobriety (complete abstinence from drugs and alcohol) feels really different than that. Sobriety is an energy. It is more than what it is not. It is something unto itself.

As a witch I am interested in and familiar with energies. I feel that my sobriety grows, it builds and gains momentum, the longer I am sober. Three years sober has more sober energy than two years did. I am interested in exploring this energy, of getting to know my sobriety on an energetic level.

I also think this conceptual shift is important. Sobriety is always positioned as absence, lack. It is constructed as a neutral, natural, plain state of being. Intoxication is seen as the introduction of something special, an exceptional experience. But for me, sobriety is exceptional. It has weight and depth. It has electric sparkles of energy. It has momentum, radiance, texture, heat. As an addict-alcoholic who was unable to string together days of sobriety, the state of ongoing sobriety is not natural, it is exceptional.

I want to talk about sobriety as more than what we don't do. Not drinking and not doing drugs is literally the smallest part of it. Sobriety is so much more than that. I am tired of only hearing representations of sobriety that describe it as a struggle, that describe the endless allure of alcohol and how we all secretly wish we could be normal and drink. That may be true for some people but I can tell you, for a fact, that as an alcoholic/addict I could never stay sober if that is what sobriety was for me. It has to be more and blessedly, it is, so much more.

Sobriety is memory, is presence, is long visible nights and clear warm mornings. Sobriety is growth, sobriety is change, sobriety is the expanse of sky and the heat of the summer sun on my skin. Sobriety is my feet against my bike pedals and knowing I can ride as long as I like, I am not being pulled and compelled toward the liquor store with a million little stories about how this time it will be different. Sobriety is freedom, the freedom to act, to remember and be accountable for my actions, to choose, to decide, to learn from what has happened, to be there, to be where I want to be.

Sobriety is ripe fruit weighing down branches, the sparkle of light across white snow or dark water, the crisp cool air. Sobriety is peace, promise, hope, joy, pleasure, presence, possibility, freedom, freedom, freedom. Sobriety is an energy, alive and full.

Young and Sober on a Friday Night

A typical Friday night for me looks like this: At around 9:30 pm a large group of friends and I squeeze our way into a coffee shop. There is barely enough room for us. Sometimes we try all four coffee shops that are open in the area before settling on the one that seems to have the most space. Often we can't share a table. Frequently some of us are just awkwardly standing around. At 11 pm the coffee shop closes and we are asked to leave. This time of year, it being winter and very cold, we can't just hang out in a park. Having nowhere else to go, we usually call it a night.

This may seem strange. My neighborhood is crawling with large, spacious bars, some with multiple rooms and even floors. They stay open past 2 am. These are the places where most people my age spend their Friday nights. They are places to socialize, talk, hang out and meet new people. They are places which my friends and I experience as somewhere between alienating and dangerous. They are not accessible spaces for us.

My friends and I are addicts and alcoholics in recovery. We don't drink and we can't drink safely. Some of us have long term sobriety and no desire to return to drinking. Some of us are trying desperately to string together days without a relapse. We range in age from our late teens to early thirties. There are a lot of us.

We go to 12 step meetings. We support each other. We know that staying sober is life or death for us. We do not have the privilege of being social drinkers. We never have and never will have the ability to moderate our drinking or drug use. At the same time, we are young people who want to have fun. We want places to hang out and talk and laugh together. We want spaces that are safe, inclusive and accessible to us. For some of us in early recovery entering spaces in which alcohol is everywhere is dangerous. For some of us, it is just really uncomfortable to be around so many drunk people.

In a culture where Friday night means drinking, where having fun means drinking, where socializing means drinking, where being young means drinking, where do we fit in? In a culture where an invitation to get to know someone sounds like "Can I get you a drink?" and that drink could land us in the hospital, in jail or worse, how do we get to know people? When all the coffee shops close by 11pm, where do sober people go to hang out and socialize on a Friday night?

The current culture of intoxication as the standard for having fun is simply not good enough. It's not accessible to a lot of people. For addicts and alcoholics who are trying to remain sober it is dangerous. It contributes to the myth that life in sobriety is boring and dull (it is not). What is boring and dull is the assumption that everyone wants to drink on a Friday night, that everyone equates drinking with having a good time, that there is nothing else we can do for fun.

Sober alternatives to nightlife are beginning to pop up. In Ann Arbor, Michigan Brillig Dry Bar recently opened. In Portland, Oregon, 4th Dimension hosts sober dance parties. Based in Nottingham, UK, Sobar describes itself as "the alcohol-free alternative bar venue for everyone; offering superb food, drink and original entertainment in a vibrant and welcoming environment."

Unfortunately for my friends and I there is nothing like this happening in our city. The number of young people in recovery is large. The number of sober spaces to socialize in the evening and at night is almost non-existent. I believe that a cultural shift is starting, as evidenced by the sober spaces that are beginning to appear. The shift is slow and the need is great. I can only hope that it gains momentum.

For the social drinkers reading this, maybe the need for sober spaces seems irrelevant to your life. If that is so I think it only proves the pervasiveness of intoxication culture. What if drinking were one of many possible things to do on a Friday or Saturday night, instead of *the* thing? What if all of us had more options? I want to imagine a world with more possibilities. I want to imagine a world where addicts and alcoholics in recovery are supported and welcomed. I want to imagine a world where my friends and I aren't left out in the cold.

Sobriety and Sex

I want to talk about sex, and desire, and consent (and lack of it) and hypersexuality and demisexuality and intoxication culture and my life. I want to tell you that for years I would get drunk with the intention of hooking up and I did and I thought I was empowered and proud but actually a lot of the time I was really sad. I want to tell you about coming to naked in various places and having no idea where I am or why I'm naked but being able to assume that I had sex. Not knowing if I used a condom or who I had sex with. Having guys approach me on the street who know details about me and clearly have had sex with me but I literally do not recognize them and have no idea who they are.

I want to tell you that I used to tell guys I'm "not like the other girls" (internalized misogyny) and that I was down to fuck and I wanted sex just like they did and I wouldn't get all attached or try to be their girlfriend. Then we'd be fucking and they wouldn't kiss me because they "don't kiss sluts" and I would start crying and screaming and freaking out.

I used booze to access my desire, to perform my desire, to pretend my desire, to find a way to get close to another human, to find a crack in the perpetual loneliness, to feel a body next to mine. I said I loved sex and I guess in some ways I did but I think deep down I just wanted company. But I thought, who would spend time with a drunk like me? Who would bother, if they weren't getting something out of it themselves? I was hypersexual, treated booze and drugs and fucking pretty much the same, I needed something, I needed more, I needed to get out of myself. I needed to escape. But I would usually break down crying because the pain of my existence was way too fucking much.

Now, in sobriety, I have found that I am demisexual. That my hypersexuality was trauma fueled and performance and desperation and seeking and that sex was the closest thing I could get to love, care, attention. I never wanted to be that cliché and at the time I insisted I wasn't but looking back, oh my god, I was so sad and so unhappy. These days my sexuality is slow. It is so slow. I can't rush it or force it. I fall for people based on their sparkling personalities. I never realize I think someone is a babe until I've known them for awhile. I feel so much pressure from a sex-obsessed and booze-fueled culture to be fast and ready. I feel like my slow moving desire is interpreted as a lack of desire. I feel like my queer identity is frequently invalidated because I don't like to get drunk and hook up, and I don't like to fuck until I get to know someone and feel comfortable and safe (and that can take a long time).

One of the questions I get most frequently from people considering or trying to get sober is how do you manage dating and sex? People feel like sobriety is a dating and sexual death sentence. And honestly, I feel like this says more about our sexual and dating cultures (and how dysfunctional they are) than it does about sobriety. I reassure them and tell them that I haven't had trouble dating and having sex in sobriety, that the majority of people I've dated (meeting them on OkCupid or in 'real' life) have been cool with my sobriety and cool to go on dates with me sober. I won't go on a date where the other person is drinking or using because we won't be on the same wavelength and I won't engage sexually with someone who has been drinking or using because I care about consent and I won't take that risk. But I have dated and had sex with a bunch of people who are not sober in an ongoing way and it's been cool.

Sex is awkward and it's like relearning everything all over again. It's consent on a whole new level and really trying to navigate my own desire and the other person's. It's awkward and I have learned to embrace the awkward, to name it, point it out, be honest about it, laugh about it. I find this approach to be honest and fun and it takes the pressure off sex as a performance. It helps me to just feel real about what's actually going on. It's 100% different from the drunk sex I used to have.

So yes, dating and sex are possible in sobriety. And I have found that even non-sober people are down for sober sex and dating if that's what their date is into. It helps to be very upfront from the beginning about your boundaries with this stuff so that anyone who would not be cool with it won't even bother to try to date you.

But it isn't all easy, in fact it's harder and more work to be sober and present and navigating consent and trauma and triggers and desires and all of that. And it's also hard in a (queer) culture that is saturated in booze and has some pretty fucked up standards about sex. It's hard to navigate this and to be honest and to carve out and create our own spaces and ways of being. It's hard and painful and alienating and exciting and rewarding and incredible work.

Abstinence and Harm Reduction Are Not Opposites

Complete abstinence and harm reduction approaches to addiction recovery are usually positioned as mutually exclusive and in opposition to each other. We are two groups of non-normative substance users / addicts who have different approaches, different support needs and different access needs. What we have in common is being on the 'outside' in the context of intoxication culture. The standard of desirability and normalcy in intoxication culture is moderate, controlled drinking and using (of certain drugs). Addicts, sober or not, fail to live up to this standard. We share the stigma of being addicts (in different ways) and we share the alienation of not fitting into intoxication culture (in different ways).

I would like to build bridges and connections between abstinence and harm reduction communities by developing solidarity, learning how we can be supportive of each other, recognizing our shared struggles and honouring our differences. For me, harm reduction in terms of switching substances or moderating does not work. I am unable to stop or moderate and which intoxicating substance I use doesn't matter; I will use addictively. That doesn't mean harm reduction is not a part of my life. I use condoms when I have penetrative sex and I wear a helmet when I ride my bike. These things are harm reduction. Abstinence is also a form of harm reduction; it completely eliminates the harm of drug/alcohol use, and it's the only form of harm reduction with relation to drugs and alcohol the can work for me personally.

I am an addict-alcoholic who is sober (abstinent). I advocate for sober spaces in community (where no one is turned away for drinking/using prior to arriving). I do a lot of work to support addicts/alcoholics trying to get sober. I also believe that all drugs should be decriminalized and that addicts, alcoholics and drug users should not be stigmatized. I believe that harm reduction information and materials, safe injection sites and needle exchanges are essential and save lives. My solidarity is first and foremost with addicts and alcoholics (using or not) before it is with sober people who are sober by choice.

Intoxication culture would like me to forget where I come from, would like me, now that I am not so visibly 'crazy', to drink normally (which is impossible) or to at least minimize the visibility of my sobriety. And intoxication culture would like me to distance myself from addicts and alcoholics in active use, to add to their stigmatization and isolation. I refuse to do that. I am continuously challenging myself and working to find ways to protect my own sobriety and recovery while also honouring, respecting, supporting and working with addicts and alcoholics whose paths are different from mine.

Addiction Is a Disability Justice Issue

Addiction is a disability justice issue. Access needs for addicts are a disability justice issue.

Addicts are not failures, fuck ups, creating our own self-imposed misery. This narrative is ableist. We are struggling with something that is beyond our control. We need support and understanding not judgement and stigma.

I was invited to speak on a panel at a disability justice event about my short film *Resurrection* which is about my experience as an alcoholic-addict. When I got to the event there was a bar (which no one had warned me about) and I was handed a drink ticket for being on the panel. How about you don't hand the sober alcoholic here to speak about addiction through a disability justice lens a DRINK TICKET?

When communities only have events that serve alcohol, these communities can't claim to prioritize accessibility. An event that serves alcohol can't claim to be 'completely accessible'. Events are rarely 'completely accessible' but transparency about access is important. List in your access info whether or not alcohol with be served at the event. This helps people make informed decisions for themselves and it also decentres intoxication culture as an invisible norm.

Referring yourself to as a 'TV junkie' or using addiction in a metaphorical way is ableist language. Assuming that everyone relates to drugs and alcohol in the way that you do is ableist thinking. Using alcohol as a common denominator that bonds people together is ableist. Assuming that fun, relaxation, celebration, summer, Friday nights or anything else necessarily includes drinking and making comments that imply such is ableist.

Intoxication culture is violent, ableist and oppressive. Intoxication culture produces a standard and leaves no space for those who can't live up to it. Receiving the message that I am not normal because I can't drink, every day, in endless micro-aggressions, exclusions and assumptions is bullshit. Undermining and undoing intoxication culture is a disability justice project.

Intoxication Culture is a Bore

I often come across discussions online in which sober people are trying to find ways to continue to enjoy socializing and going out now that they have stopped drinking. Feedback ranges from becoming super into drinking sodas and fancy drinks to hiding the fact that you're not drinking to giving up on nightlife and parties all together. The common thread that runs through these discussions is the idea that sober people need to find ways to adapt and adjust or else we need to give up and retreat. We are the sober ones, the odd ones out, and it is up to us to find ways to fit in.

Looking at this discourse, it reminds me of homonormativity. How can we, as queer people, fit into a straight world? How can we blend in seamlessly, get married and join the military, and prove to everyone that we are just like straight people? Critics of homonormativity rightly point out that there is nothing wrong with being queer and that it's okay if being queer doesn't look like being straight. Critics of homonormativity rightly change the question from "How can we be more like straight people?" to "Why is the world so intolerant of us as we are?"

Likewise, I would like to shift the questions around sober people living within the dominant intoxication culture. Instead of asking "How can I continue to fit in among my drinking friends now that I don't drink?" I would like to ask "Why is having fun only understood as drinking?" Instead of feeling like there is something wrong with me, like I'm boring or a buzzkill, I would like to consider why every single social event includes alcohol consumption as a default. Sure, drinking is fun for some people. For others it is dangerous and alienating. So, in the interest of having accessible, inclusive communities, can we imagine various and differing ideas of fun?

Here's a shocking idea: Drinking as synonymous with fun and socializing does not have to be the norm. The idea that we should include drinking with all social events is a social construction and it's an oppressive social construction. Things could be different. Drinking could be a part of some events and not others. Coffee and tea, dinner without the wine, dance parties without the booze, these could be common, normal Friday and Saturday night occurrences. For many people, especially but not limited to those who are sober in an ongoing way, these would be welcome.

Within the narrative that drinking is the normal way to have fun is the implicit idea that those of us who can't or don't drink are not normal. There is something wrong with us. We are deficient. Therefore, it is on us to adapt. Normal people doing normal drinking shouldn't have to accommodate us because it is not their fault that we are not normal. I refuse to buy into this script. My difference does not make me deficient. My inability to drink does not make me abnormal. Your drinking culture is not and should not be the only option.

I love being a sober addict. I love my life. I love my friends. I love my community. I love the sober culture that I am a part of. Yes, it is a culture. A rich, complex and diverse culture. We have our own ways to socialize, celebrate and have fun. We do not feel deficient or lacking in this. The problem arises only when we are involved with dominant intoxication culture. Lots of sober people don't mind being the only one not drinking, don't mind that the majority of events include drinking. And lots of sober people do mind, do feel weird and excluded, and do leave the party early. And for lots of sober people, like those who are early in recovery or struggling with their sobriety, the dominant intoxication culture is dangerous.

I don't want to learn how to blend in with drinkers. I don't want to learn how to be a sober person having fun on their terms. I love my sobriety and my sober culture. I do not wish I could drink. I do not want to 'fit in'.

But I am tired of intoxication culture dominating all social and community events. I am tired of drinking being assumed and implicit. It is not my responsibility as a sober addict to adjust myself to your intoxication culture. If you believe in accessibility, inclusivity and justice then it is your responsibility as a normative drinker to make space for people who can't and don't drink. Your way of living is not the only way. Your idea of fun is not the only idea. There are other people in your communities who have different relationships to drinking than you do. It's time for things to change.

12 Step Witches

When I was 25 I decided to "take a break from drinking" again. I had done this before but I was never able to stay stopped. I knew I was an alcoholic but I really didn't know what could be done about it. I had heard about 12 step programs but my impression of them was that they were super-religious (Christian) and populated exclusively by old men. I assume I got this impression from representations I had seen on TV and in the media. As a queer femme politicized witch I really didn't see how it would work for me so I never considered going.

When I decided to "take a break from drinking" again I was fortunate to mention this to an acquaintance who was also queer and politicized. She told me that I should check out 12 step meetings. She told me this was how she got and stayed sober. She told me about some local meetings and I went. This was three years ago. I am still sober and my life has completely changed. 12 steps programs saved my life. They are still a central and essential part of my life today. I could never put into words my gratitude for the culture, community, fellowship, support, spirituality, change, recovery and sobriety that 12 steps programs have given me.

12 step programs are spiritual, not religious. I have lots of friends who are in 12 step programs and are spiritual in all sorts of ways. I know spiritual atheists, those who connect with the universe, 12 steps witches, those who see spirituality in community and activism, people who connect with organized religion, people who have reconnected with the spirituality of their families, people who reject that spirituality and find one of their own.

12 step cultures make space for talking about and taking seriously spirituality in a way that mainstream culture (where I live) doesn't. I love that about 12 step cultures. I love that my 12 step friends, witchy or not, make space for, encourage and understand why my spiritual path is so important to me. I love that my witchy friends who are not in 12 steps programs make space for my 12 step approach to spirituality. I love the hybrid of witchcraft and 12 steps that guides me and sustains me in my everyday life. Blessed be.

Learning to let the Love in

Capricorns get better with age. I'm 28. Please don't compare me to cheese or wine. I'm a sober vegan. I'm happy. Right now I am happy and full of gratitude and trusting the universe. I am learning how to love myself. Learning that I am loved. Fear has kept me from being able to accept love from myself or others. But right now I am willing to surrender fear and step into the profound truth of love. Today a friend of mine told me I am an astonishing person. This evening I got a sincere thank you for my service in someone else's recovery. Tonight my roommate told me my book made her cry and that she loved it. My life is full. I am growing into who I am meant to be. I am willing to begin to let the love in, to begin to believe I am worthy of it. I am happy. And I am grateful.

Inherent Worth

I'm was doing this trauma group for a while and we did a CBT exercise where we broke down troubling thoughts until we got to an underlying 'root' thought. The root thought was 'I'm worthless'. We then were challenged to think of evidence against this thought. I told the facilitators that I felt this was a trap. Whatever I say to prove my worth is external and can be taken away. They knew me so they suggested I put down that I'm three years sober and in a relationship. I asked "What if I get drunk tomorrow? What if my partner leaves me? What about when I was drunk and alone, sitting on the street in the middle of the day? Did I have no worth then?" They told me that I'm not there anymore and I don't give myself enough credit for where I am now (which is true). But they couldn't answer my question. What about people who are now where I was? What about drunks, fuck ups, people who are down and out? Are they worthless?

I realized that the only thing I could write for evidence against my worthlessness is that everyone has inherent worth. Everyone. Myself included. Because if I attach my worth to any external thing, to anything, it is dangerous. If I attach my worth to my sobriety, my partner, my creative work, trying to be a good person, anything, it is dangerous. Because what if I don't have those things anymore? And what if, in a desperate, frenzied attempt to hold on to those things, I lose them? I need to believe that just by being I am worthy of safety, love, happiness, dignity. It was surprising for me to realize this, but I attach so much of my worth to my sobriety, and who I have been able to become in my sobriety. I have very little compassion for the person I used to be. As much as it is true that my sobriety is the foundation of my life, the most important thing in my life, it cannot be the reason I believe I have worth. Everyone has worth. No matter what our circumstances are.

Reminder

I can do healing things for myself without turning it into a form of self harm by demanding perfection.

I Don't Need to Fuck You to Prove that I'm Queer

I went to an event today for queer and trans survivors of violence. It brought up some surprising stuff for me. I am a survivor of a lot of violence, including a lot of sexual violence. Something I don't talk about a lot is that I have been sexually assaulted by women. There are a couple instances. The most 'serious' is that I was drugged and raped by a woman when I was 17. She was 21. I have been coerced into sexual activity by women and queer people multiple times, including this instance when I was 17, in which I showed a lot of hesitancy and she finally drugged me. It just clicked in my head today that women have pressured me to have sex with them, using the fact that I am a femme polysexual queer person against me. Basically, my queerness has come under question and I have been expected to engage in sexual activity to prove my queerness. I feel like this stuff never gets talked about. I saw an article floating around Facebook recently called something like "if you only date men you don't get to call yourself queer" (which I didn't read) and I remember a scene in Orphan Black where a woman tells her partner it's obvious she hasn't been with other women (because of her 'skill level') and her queerness comes into question. And I hear stuff like this all the time, especially directed towards femmes and polysexual queers. I just realized today that this stuff is not only "biphobic" but actually really sexually violent. I am sexually and romantically attracted to and desire intimacy with women, femmes, nonbinary people, masculine people and men (and probably other people who don't fit under any of those labels). Beyond that, my understandings of sex and love are explicitly political, critical and QUEER. I just realized today how much baggage I am carrying around from being told, subtly and directly, to prove it, and how this has been the framework of multiple experiences of sexual violence in my life.

Femme Friendship is Better Than Jealousy

Jealousy robs me of my need to witness and affirm other femmes. Jealousy robs me of my need for solidarity and friendship with other femmes. Healing happens in femme friendship. So much healing.

Femme is Defiance

Today, after changing my hair colour from green to blue, I put on a little black dress, some burgundy lipstick and an old pair of sneakers. I was feeling really good in my body, in my gender and in myself. I knew that a lot of people would think my dress was too short and that my bright blue hair was 'asking for attention' but I knew those people would be wrong. I knew that this femme embodiment is a hard won confidence, a willingness to face down sexual violence every single day in order to dress the way that most authentically represents who I am.

Femme is not public property. Femme does not need your comments and approval. Femme is not an invitation to talk to me. Femme is not an invitation for your sexually violent behaviour. Femme is not 'asking for it'. Femme is not about you. Femme is about the femme being femme.

Femmes are not interchangeable. Femmes are not an endless array of exciting new options. Femmes are not here to fulfill your sexual fantasies. Femmes are not here to entertain you. Femmes are not here to take care of you. Femmes don't owe you any fucking thing. Not a smile. Not our time. Not conversation. Not an explanation. We don't owe you shit.

Today, feeling super good about being a femme, even in the face of the nonstop misogynist femmephobic bullshit I experience, I took a selfie. I used the timer app on my phone so I could get my whole outfit. I captioned the photo: Femme is defiance. Then I left my house, not giving a fuck if my dress was too short.

I got less than a block before a man started following me. He yelled "Excuse me" and caught up to me. Thinking maybe I had dropped something or that maybe he had some legitimate reason for talking to me, I stopped. But then he started saying the usual shit "This is really weird but I just blew off my friend to come talk to you. You just look so interesting. I just had to come say hi. Where are you going?" He reached out and stroked my arm, running his fingers across my skin.

Scared, exhausted, fed up, I just mumbled something about being on my way to run some errands and tried to speed up. He just kept on talking to me, at me, about me, paying no heed to my obvious discomfort. I looked around, weighed out my options, tried to figure out how to get rid of him. I wanted to tell him to leave me the fuck alone but times when I stood up for myself only to have the situation escalate into "You look like a dirty whore anyway" "Stuck up bitch" "You're fucking ugly" and other violent, scary things played over in my mind.

Finally I just told him that I don't know him and the fact that he was following me and talking to me was really weird. He told me that he was just trying to be nice and I told him that he was actually sexually harassing me. Fortunately he just said he wasn't but then backed off. I hurried away feeling awful.

When I talk to my femme friends, I hear stories about fucked up shit like this happening to them constantly. It happens to me constantly. Femmes who are also Black, Indigenous or people of colour, femmes who are trans, especially trans women, femmes who are gender nonconforming, femmes who are sex workers, femmes who are homeless, femmes who are addicted, femmes who are fat and femmes who are disabled get it even worse. Trans women of colour are murdered for daring to embody their femininity in public.

I am so angry. I am so exhausted. I am so sick of this bullshit. I honour the wisdom, bravery and brilliance of all femme, feminine and feminized people. We do not deserve this. This shit is not our fault. The fact that we continue to be our own femme selves, whether in our bedrooms, on the internet or on the street, in the face of such violence, constantly inspires and amazes me.

Femme is courage. Femme is daring. Femme is defiance.

Disappearing Daughter

Keeping family secrets is like poison. Everyone wants a pretty picture. Slap a band aid on it. I am the disappearing daughter. The crazy one. The one who made such a big deal out of everything. I tried so hard for so long to be good and what did it get me? I can't keep your secrets anymore.

Pisces Super Moon

This Pisces Super Moon is working hard on me. So many issues bubbling to the surface for healing and integration.

Perfectionism, martyrdom linked with childhood neglect and abuse. Alcoholic dad workoholic mom... Generations of trauma and alcoholism/addiction.

The self-loathing that comes out of that. Thinking I am not a 'good person'... and the way that even social justice work is all tied up with this stuff for me. I went vegetarian at age six... Obsessed all throughout my childhood about animal products... Terrified of being wrong, causing harm, being bad...

And the way 'good' also meant 'respectful' 'compliant'... not saying no to my pedophile grandfather...

(And then the shadow of all this martyrdom and perfectionism: the 'I don't give a fuck about anything or anyone' active alcoholism days where I caused harm on the regular, trying so hard to be 'tough', 'bad', badder than the people who hurt me, waking up sick, hung over... Full of shame... So back to the bottle quick.)

Intimacy issues... Terrified of letting people get close... I usually have one close relationship, this person sees the real Clementine... Everyone else I keep at a distance, it is so hard for me to let people in.

Tip toeing around in fear... Terrified to let my guard down... Terrified that deep down, ultimately, I am bad, unworthy, unloveable, not good enough and if I'm not careful, people will find out.

Feeling like I need to 'trick' or manipulate people into loving me, not trusting that they could really love me for me, imperfect and human and traumatized.

Pisces Super Moon digging up all the buried shit. Telling me now is the time to offer unconditional love and forgiveness to myself, to honour the inherent worthiness of every single being, to HEAL, to heal, to heal, to let go and to trust

That I am loved.

That I am safe.

That I am worthy.

Now to re-pot my plant friends who are outgrowing their pots...

Wishing

I'm wishing for your joy, for your peace. I'm wishing you find love, I'm wishing that you heal. I'm wishing that the secret pain gets the light and love and healing that it needs. I'm wishing for your freedom, hoping you are free. <3 <3 <3

Secrets

Venus is coming out of retrograde tomorrow. What have I learned? What have I learned?

My hair is turquoise because I mixed the dye with conditioner. I am painting my nails with clear sparkly nail polish.

I have been so utterly disconnected from my body. I don't masturbate hardly ever anymore because SHAME.

Trauma trauma trauma. The longer I am sober the more the memories freak me out. All that sex I had when I was drunk... it was so fucking unhealthy. It was sex as self-harm. It was all I knew to do.

My heart. My heart. My heart.

But maybe I can't pretend anymore. Maybe I have arrived. Maybe this really is my life now.

Drinking hot water with lemon. Listening to sad songs.

Lately what has been coming to the surface is... secrets.

I have never been able to have sex with femmes. All my life I have been attracted to femmes. My first sexuality was GAY. And I was a closeted nine year old dyke in a small town.

When I came out I experienced so much old-school homophobia. Got called a dyke every day, told I was going to burn in hell, called disgusting, 'don't touch the dyke you might catch something', 'something smells like fish' etc.

But I remember kissing my first girlfriend in the halls of that shitty high school and feeling for the first time in my body real pleasure, real desire.

But sex as I have always known it has been violence. That's the truth. My first sexual experience was my grandfather forcibly making out with me.

After that it was unwanted hands and being cornered and I learned to like it because I had no other choice.

But with femmes... all I ever wanted was to be with femmes. All I ever wanted was to have honest, consensual sex with femmes. And not just sex, sex with feelings like respect, care, kindness, consideration. That's my desire, that's what turns me on.

But growing up exposed to pornography, the fantasies of heterosexual men and trying to interpret my queer desire through that. And that combined with childhood incestuous sexual abuse. And that combined with always seeing and knowing that sex was DANGER.

And then... the shame of being in love with my best friend. The shame of knowing she would be disgusted if she knew. It made me feel disgusting, and invasive, and violent and gross.

And then when I came out, that's how I was painted... 'don't turn around, we're changing!', 'if you're gay does that mean you're attracted to yourself?'... The way my friends would suddenly pull away if we touched by accident, the looks they gave me, always suspicious, accusing.

All we ever did was talk about crushes (on boys) but my crushes, which I did have, but could never say, were already painted as bad, gross, unwanted.

Monstrous queer desire.

Oh yeah I internalized this shit. And by the time I dropped out of high school and moved to Toronto and found other queers I was thoroughly fucked up.

My first serious long term girlfriend and I never had sex. We did everything else. I was super turned on by her, super into her, loved grinding against her and making out with her and holding her in my arms at night. She absolutely disarmed me with her beauty. Femme for femme 100%. But I was terrified. Terrified of doing something wrong, hurting her, crossing a line.

After we broke up I heard that she went around telling people that I wasn't really queer because we never had sex.

And then there were the times that I was sexually assaulted by women... three times in a row... two of which qualify as rape but ohmygod I couldn't deal with that or call it that or think about that because I had this delusional idea that women were supposed to be safe.

So it was easier to just be with men and play the hetero script and yes, be sexually assaulted frequently, and yes, play into their fantasies and learn to like it and learn to fall desperately in love and be some kind of happy there.

I am polysexual and I do have genuine attraction/desire for men and masculine people but most of my experiences have been utterly fucked up. And to be honest I was sleeping with dudes because I hated myself for being a queer femme and a survivor of incest and a fucking failure at the only thing my little child-self wanted: to get out and be queer and be happy.

Now I'm almost 30. I've been queer my whole life. I've been out of the closet half of it. And I have never been able to genuinely, soberly, honestly, without terror, engage in sexuality with women.

I have had some queer sex with nonbinary femmes and queer men... not a lot of it, and not without its complications. I have had some queer sex with women... but again, not without tons of baggage and mostly not without booze.

My partner is a nonbinary femme assigned male at birth and I am a nonbinary femme assigned female at birth. We get read as a straight couple and the heterosexual matrix has its impact on us. The internalized misogyny and queerphobia that is embedded in my body is not activated when the world pretends that we are straight.

I want to find and uproot imposed heterosexuality and male supremacy from my body. I want to be free of the legacy of cissexist transphobic queerphobic femmephobic misogynist violence. I want my partner and I to be able to shine in our queerness.

And one day I want to be able to explore sexuality with women and other femmes. I want to be able to be present to my desires without feeling like a creep or a pervert, without shutting down and shutting off. I want to dig deep inside of myself and find the poison and get rid of it.

All of this just makes me want to cry. My last girlfriend thought I wasn't into her because I move so fucking slow. And when I tried to explain all of this it made no sense and it made me feel like I had to prove my queerness.

Just the other day I was reading *How Poetry Saved My Life* by Amber Dawn. The unashamed way she speaks of queer desire made me realize that I am full of internalized queerphobia, internalized misogyny and so much fucking trauma. And I was jealous and aching reading her words, grieving the experiences I've never had, grieving all the femmes who wondered why I wouldn't just go for it. Mourning my sexuality which was fucking butchered by childhood sexual abuse.

Oh well. Venus comes out of retrograde tomorrow. What have I learned?

The Bottom of a Lake: Trauma, Pain and Chronic Sickness

My body is hijacked. Migraine coming on, can feel the blur of sickness, the slur of tired pulling on my body. Go to bed for days. It's summer, bright and hot. My instagram and Facebook feeds are full of pictures of beaches, parks and bike rides. I want so badly to be a part of it. I feel the dread of regret for wasting even a moment of summer, because the winters are so deadly long. But I am like a stone sinking into deep water; my mind is a mess of confusion and the tangle of seaweed at the bottom of a lake. I am the oblivion of sickness and I am here again.

The more I learn about trauma, the more everything makes sense. Unfortunately childhood trauma has a long-lasting impact on basically everything. Unfortunately no amount of positive thinking is going to unthink the way that trauma has settled into my body. Unfortunately no matter how badly I want to 'get better' I am stuck in the mud of chronic fatigue and sickness. I am drowning in cortisol and my body can't get up from under it. I am exhausted.

At a disability studies conference I went to, a speaker whose name I don't remember said "Trauma is not what we mean when we talk about desiring disability." My eyes stung with tears because, yes, those words are true. There is a linear narrative of recovery that means we must always be moving away from trauma, always getting a little better than we were the day before. And I wish that were true. But sometimes it's two steps forward and three steps back. And sometimes it's no steps forward because it's hard to walk at all when you are at the bottom of a lake.

My Body That Doesn't Exist

My desire is like a person I know riding the same train as me but I don't realize it until I'm almost at my destination and I've been staring at them blankly the whole time. My desire, when it comes, is a surprise and often, an inconvenience. Often, it doesn't come at all.

I have felt the demanding hands of lovers, dates, partners, who wanted, who expected, who pleaded for my desire. I have felt the hands which did not notice or did not care that my desire wasn't there. My inability to summon up desire has been used against me, used as evidence that I am not really queer, used as evidence that I am a liar, used as evidence that I am crazy or selfish or not into a person I really am into.

Especially because sometimes my desire does come. Especially because sometimes it is vast and expansive. Especially because I can't control or predict when it will.

Especially because I have a history of so many sex partners, of so much drunk and dissociated sex, so if I could summon up desire then, and I could, then why can't I here, now, when it's safe.

A person who isn't crazy in the way that I am crazy would not understand this. The body I had then was on loan, it was a body like a marionette that I could use when I needed to in order to feel something, but it wasn't this body that I call home. This body that I call home is not a body. It's a body that never existed.

I mourn the body I never had. I imagine this body, a ghostly impression just out of reach of the body that is actually here. I beckon and call and try to will it into existence. But contact with this body is fleeting. Contact with wanting is fleeting.

Sometimes it does come.

When my desire hits it's a flush, a rush, a rainstorm. But it is always too late.

When it comes, it comes and when it doesn't, well, it doesn't.

I wish the world would slow down and give my desire a chance to catch up.

Trauma Meets Grad School

For the past three years or so I have been focusing mainly on my recovery from trauma and addiction. Since getting sober and making the decision to make my healing my main priority, my life has changed drastically. During this time I also discovered disability justice communities and began the work of loving my madness. Living in an ableist culture, I had a lot of unlearning to do. Over the past three years I have begun to politicize my experience as a traumatized, disabled, sick, addict and psychiatric survivor. I have begun to understand that it is not that I am 'crazy', 'lazy', 'melodramatic', 'fucked up', 'pathetic', 'making too much of a big deal out of things', 'difficult', or 'a failure' but that my brain and body experience things differently than a lot of people, due mainly to my experiences of physical, emotional and sexual violence, in childhood and adulthood.

It has really been so much work learning to love myself. I can't say that the work is even close to done. But I have come so far. I have to admit though that driving my recovery was a belief that if I worked hard enough, one day I wouldn't be crazy anymore. I believed that if I kept doing the work and seeking the help that one day my brain and body would more closely resemble the brains and bodies of people who are not traumatized. A counselor I was seeing noticed how hard I was pushing myself toward this goal and asked me the question "What if you never 'get better'?" She was trying to help me understand that complex PTSD is thought of as a permanent disability. That I may lessen my symptoms, get better at managing them, but I may not ever have a brain like one that didn't experience childhood sexual abuse. When she asked me that I was angry and horrified. I told her the truth as I felt it then. I told her that if I thought I had to be this way forever I would kill myself. I couldn't imagine the point of living this life with no finish line in sight, no 'after', no chance at being normal.

I had known I felt this way, but to say it out loud was something else. I realized that, despite all the work in recovery I had done, despite how much I believed in disability justice and valuing difference, I was deeply affected by internalized ableism. I hated myself for being crazy and I believed that the only point to being alive was the sliver of hope that one day I might not have to be crazy anymore. The more that I thought about this, the more I realized how fucked up it was. The more I thought about it, the more I realized that every narrative I ever heard about trauma, even within disability justice circles, was always about moving away from trauma. Trauma was always collapsed into its source: violence. Trauma was always a negative. Trauma was always something to not be anymore.

But what if I'm like this for the rest of my life?

I recently started grad school. This is my first time doing anything full time in over three years. For my Masters project I want to explore some of these questions. I want to consider the reasons behind the imperative to not be traumatized anymore. I want to ask the question "Can we love trauma?" Can we love trauma so that we can love the traumatized? Can we engage with trauma in a way other than movement away from it? Can we consider what trauma might offer us, what trauma might teach us? Can we consider that trauma can still be a liveable, loveable, worthy life? These are the questions I am setting forth to guide my research, with the intention set in my heart to answer yes. Yes we can love trauma. Yes we can listen to trauma. Yes I can love my traumatized body and mind. Yes I don't have to kill myself if I'm like this forever.

And so, I am in grad school, a couple weeks in. I am writing and reading and researching. I am swamped and I am struggling. Like I said, I haven't been in school for three years. People told me that grad school was intense, but I had no idea that it would be this hard. What I didn't realize, what I should have realized by now, is that grad school would affect me differently because of my trauma. Yes, it's stressful and I guess that's just the way grad school is. (I would argue that it shouldn't be this way. I would argue that the level of stress imposed on students is ableist and oppressive and that we shouldn't have to feel so stressed out in order to learn and work on our ideas.) But the thing about me and my traumatized bodymind is that when I experience stress, I don't just feel stressed, I feel *unsafe*.

Since starting school my moods have been all over the place. I've been waking up depressed, having extreme anxiety all day. My hyper-vigilance is through the roof, constantly assessing what I perceive to be risks. The urgency is real. It feels like my whole life is on the line. I am experiencing suicidal ideation, intrusive thoughts of self-injury and full blown self-loathing. I hate to write these things because I don't want people to worry or misunderstand. I don't want this to constitute an emergency because it is not. The thing about me and my traumatized bodymind is that I create and experience emergencies that are 'not there' in the sense that they don't exist in 'objective reality' the way that I experience them internally. The way that I experience them is very real, but they are not 'real' in the sense of mutually agreed upon 'reality'.

I have been hating myself for having this reaction. I have been struggling and hating myself for struggling. I have been desperately wishing and wanting to just 'be normal', to be stressed but not this stressed, to be stressed but still feel safe. I have been resisting this trauma response, pushing it down, shutting it out, hating it. And then of course it dawned on me. I want to do a research project about how we don't have to run from trauma. I want to do a research project where I allow my trauma to be a part of the conversation. I want to do work that allows trauma to exist. I want to exist. I want to be okay with the way that I exist. I want to make space for the fact that my brain and body respond differently. I want to honour that difference and be with it and see what it has to teach me. I want to create knowledge from this place of embodied experience. I want to write and work from my trauma, my crazy, and I want to know that it's okay.

And so it's late and I am writing this. I am writing this because it is part of my process, it is part of my work. I am writing this for every one of us who has been expected to act like we aren't feeling the way we feel, who has been pressured to pretend to have an entirely different experience, in order to survive. I am traumatized, I am crazy, I am alive and I am being honest. This is the work.

Spiritual Experiences: Valuing and Politicizing Spirituality

I am a sober addict/alcoholic and my recovery is rooted in spirituality. I am a survivor of violence who lives with C-PTSD and depression and my recovery is rooted in spirituality. I am a writer and an artist and a community organizer and a lifelong learner and my process is rooted in spirituality. When I become spirituality disconnected, I become unwell. It is dangerous for me not to centre, care for and prioritize my spiritual life.

Yet, it is easy, in the culture in which I live, to lose sight of spirituality. In a culture that understands my addiction as only a physical and mental condition, the spiritual aspect can be lost. In a culture which defines my trauma as mental illness, as biomedical reality, the spiritual element can be lost. Within the spheres of art making, political work and community organizing, I can get lost in burn out and forget to connect each action I take with my spiritual core.

It is true also that I live on stolen, colonized land, where the spiritual knowledges of the Haudenosaunee, Anishinaabe, Huron-Wendat and other Indigenous peoples of this land have been punished, repressed and appropriated. It is true that the hunger for spiritual knowing by white people is often met through violent exploitation and appropriation of other cultures. White people think we own everything, that we have the right to trample over everyone and take whatever we want. It is true that neoliberalism and capitalism have turned a search for spirituality into a personalized path of individual 'self-improvement'. Quick-fix spirituality is made easily accessible in the form of inspirational quotes, white supremacist yoga studios and astrology focused on the 'self'. Quick-fix spirituality is divorced from community, from the knowledge of our inter-connectedness, from the realities of racism, white supremacy, colonialism, global capitalism, transmisogyny, ableism and environmental destruction.

I am grateful to be involved in 12 step culture with other queer and trans people who seek and emphasize a spirituality that is connected to politics. I am grateful for the witches I know who are critical of cultural appropriation, conscious of the context of colonialism and seeking a spirituality that is committed to undoing these oppressive systems. I am grateful for queer and trans people reclaiming religious and spiritual practices. I am grateful for all the work done by Black, Indigeneous and people of colour communities in confronting and addressing white supremacy and cultural appropriation in spiritual movements.

I need spirituality in my life. I recognize that not everyone does. There are atheists and agnostics and others who are fine without spirituality in their lives.

(And there are atheists and agnostics who are also spiritual.) I sense that there are many of us with a spiritual longing who want to find ways to integrate the spiritual into our lives. The frequency of astrology blogposts and pictures of tarot readings on my social media newsfeeds suggests to me that for many of us, we are finding small ways to bring the spiritual into our lives. I am grateful for this.

I want my spiritual experiences to be as welcomed and valued as any of my other experiences. I want to be able to nurture and speak from this spiritual place of knowing. I want to enrich my spiritual practice by always keeping it interwoven with my political practice. I want my spiritual recovery and wellbeing to be considered just as valid as other approaches to recovery and wellbeing. I look forward with an open heart to more dialogue on these subjects and call more spiritual community into my life.

In the morning I light the candles on my altar. I sit before them and pray. I draw three tarot cards from my Rider-Waite-Smith deck, illustrated by Pamela Coleman Smith, and meditate upon their meaning. Throughout my day I listen to the energies around me. I feel the trees especially and when I am spiritually well I make the time to connect with them. In the warm weather, I sit or lie on the ground. Whenever I am irritated, angry, lonely, triggered or upset I try to bring myself back to my spiritual centre and act on spiritual principals. In the evening I gather with my spiritual recovery community and in a circle we pray.

My spirituality is a commitment to growth. When it is brought to my attention that I have acted oppressively, I am grateful for that opportunity to grow and to change. I am committed to learning and to challenging myself. Causing harm and refusing to acknowledge it is the surest way for me to become spiritually disconnected. Therefore, my spirituality pushes me to become a more accountable person committed to social justice and change.

Love is a Limited Resource: On Trauma and Queer Utopias

As a person who is queer and politicized and polyamorous (though currently with one partner) my newsfeeds on social media are frequently filled with statuses, tweets, posts and links which convey a particular message: Love is not a limited resource. Love should be easy and free. Jealousy and exclusivity are relics of an oppressive heterosexist capitalism. We can love, we should love, love is good and love will heal us.

There is implicit and sometimes explicit shaming of people who aren't polyamorous, who have failed at polyamory, people who are jealous, suspicious, closed hearted, people who do not love in abundance, who seem downright greedy and terrified and grasping for love. The internet announces over and over that love is everywhere, that when we are ready, it will arrive. There is no limit on love besides the limits we place on it.

But what if love really is a limited resource? I agree that it should not be. Clean water should not be a limited resource either, but it is. The reality is that what human beings need to survive and to thrive, whether it be water or love, are not freely available and accessible to all. Does it make me a capitalist to acknowledge this?

Those of us who grew up with child abuse and neglect know all too well that love can be a very limited resource. We know in our traumatized bodies, minds and hearts the desperate things we'll do to get a taste of love. We know also that what passes for love often isn't, but we have become accustomed to taking what we can get.

The internet implores me to feel love and to feel loved, to allow it to flourish where ever it will. The queer, politicized and polyamorous communities I frequent cast suspicious glances at those of us who do not, or cannot, love so freely. If I am afraid of not being loved, if I hold on too tightly, if I am afraid to let go, I may as well be a hetero-capitalist. I am certainly not embodying the ideal of a queer utopia where love exists in abundance.

I read online today that love is a feeling. I have to disagree. I have to say that for me, learning that love is not a feeling was a hard earned lesson. As a child who was never given an example of real, safe love, I became an adult having no idea what love is. A culture that convinces me love is something I 'fall into', something that happens, something I *feel*, and my starving, deprived, hungry heart, make a dangerous combination. It has taken me so long to realize that the person who put his knee on my chest and wouldn't let me breathe, who oscillated between best friend and abuser, who blamed his rage and violence on his unbelievable love for me, did not love me.

I have to agree with bell hooks when she asserts that love is an action. I remember the tears that fell on the page when I read her words. She wrote "Without justice there can be no love." She wrote "Love and abuse cannot coexist." These words were utterly painful to read because they made me wonder if I had ever in my life been loved. But they were, at the same time, utterly freeing. They opened me up to the possibility of love.

So I must hold on to these lessons. I must not let them be glossed over in a search for good feelings. Love is not a feeling. It is an action. It is a process. It is an investment in justice. It is an investment in healing. It is work. And loving a traumatized person, which so many of us are, is work. Loving as a traumatized person, which so many of us are, is work. Hard work.

What would happen if we, as queer, politicized, polyamorous communities, as communities who claim to be committed to justice, acknowledged that love, very often, is a limited resource? Love, when we understand it as an action rather than a feeling, can unfortunately be very difficult to come by for many of us. And even when opportunities for such love are available, if we are traumatized it may take us a very long time and a whole lot of work to begin to open up to that love.

What would happen if we, as queer, politicized, polyamorous communities acknowledged the regularity with which violence happens all around us? What if we stopped gaslighting people who are (justifiably) afraid? What if we held space for the legacies of trauma that so many of us carry and named loving for what it is, a daring act?

What if we acknowledged that learning to love and be loved isn't easy, but that it can be done? What if we rooted out the shaming tactics from our writing and thinking on radical, anti-capitalist queer love? What if, instead of telling survivors that love is not a limited resource, we made the terrifying admission that it is? And we continued the work of love anyway.

2016

Growth Not Shame: Still Estranged, Still Traumatized, Still Crazy in the New Year

It's the first day of 2016 and I am in a full blown depression. A bad one. It seems to have come all at once and sucked me under, but I think it was building for awhile.

This time of year is really hard for me, and for a lot of us. First Christmas emphasizes the importance of family. For me, as an incest survivor who is estranged from the majority of my family of origin, Christmas time is a striking reminder of all that I don't have. It is painful because it makes me long for connection with my family of origin, even though I know that is harmful for me. I start to internalize all the messages I have spent so long unlearning: that the problem, really, is me, that I can somehow fix everything by fixing my behaviour, by being more forgiving, by rising above it all. I know this isn't true. After years and years of trauma work, I know that I can't fix something that isn't mine to fix.

Then, in between Christmas and New Years is my birthday. This year, I didn't do much for my birthday because I have been feeling sad and overwhelmed. Christmas reminded me how alone I feel in the world and pushed me to work toward building and nurturing friendships, creating the 'chosen family' I hear so much about in queer circles. Between Christmas and my birthday I made a point to go on a number of friend dates, which were really wonderful, but also really draining.

The paradox is that, while friendship sounds like the perfect antidote to loneliness for estranged people, friendship simultaneously requires a skill set that traumatized people rarely have. We have to work extra hard at it and it takes more out of us. Or, at least this is true for me. The narrative of 'chosen family' is a cherished dream and an ideal that frequently seems impossible. On my birthday, I didn't ask anyone to do anything because the thought of it was scary and overwhelming. I was out of spoons. I couldn't be 'on'. I couldn't be so extremely emotionally vulnerable.

My Facebook filled up with sweet and thoughtful messages from community, some of which made me cry. The outpouring of internet love was meaningful to me, but also reminded me how much of my life is actually on the internet, and how hard it is for me to translate those connections into 'real life'. Several people told me how much my writing and general online presence mean to them. I was grateful for that. At the same time, all this love felt like it was coming at me from a distance and I don't know how to let it in.

And then New Years hit and so did the posts celebrating the past year and setting intentions for the next one. Along with those came the flood of pictures of people all dressed up and ready to celebrate. I spent the day in bed watching Netflix and by the evening I was wrestling with my demons hard. I was trying to gather enough spoons to go out to a party. I wanted to feel good and hopeful and happy. I did my make up and put on a dress. But I was weighted down with pain. I felt so apart from everything and everyone. I did not know how to cross that divide.

I ended up having a quiet, but sweet, night with my partner. In the morning, instead of waking up full of hope for 2016, I awoke in a deep depression. The depression persists. I canceled plans and I am now in my bed which is the only place I want to be. Netflix is on pause as I write this but I am comforted knowing that the oblivion of mindless TV is close at hand. What kind of way is this to start the new year?

I know that I am sad because I am lonely and I feel disconnected. I know that I am sad because I am estranged and I don't have anything in my life that could really be called family. I want the answer to be as simple as 'making a commitment to build friendships' but the honest truth is that it is not. The truth is that, because I am an abuse survivor, building friendships is really hard for me. The very thing that I need in order to alleviate this loneliness is also something that drains and exhausts me. Trying to build friendships is painful and triggering for me. Human relationships, intimacy, connection, this is the landscape of my trauma. There is no easy way for me to create a 'chosen family'. There is only the work.

It is good work. It is important work. It is healing, life saving, necessary work. It is also hard, awful, painful, alienating and exhausting. And I can only do so much of it before I need a break.

Someone joked with me recently that it seems like I am always on Facebook. I laughed and made some comment about it being true. But deep inside I was embarrassed. It is embarrassing to admit that the majority of human connection I experience is through a computer screen. I know my New Years resolutions should be to 'get out more' and 'spend more time with friends' and maybe even 'spend less time online' or 'watch less TV'. But the fact is that I am a traumatized, disabled, sad and crazy human being. The internet is the easiest way for me to access connection. Those connections don't fulfill me entirely. They are not what I ultimately want. But in the meantime, they help and they are better than nothing.

No matter how much I want to, I won't snap out of it. No matter how badly I want friendship to feel good and easy, it doesn't. There is no time machine or magic potion which will rewire my traumatized brain. All there is, is the work. And the internet. And Netflix. And this bed.

My new years resolution is to forgive myself for being sad and crazy. My new years resolution is to accept my limitations and work within them, stretching them only slowly, with patience and deep compassion. My new years resolution is to destroy all the ableist mythologies of what it means to have a meaningful life. My new years resolution is to make peace with the fact that 'chosen family', like 'family of origin', is at this time inaccessible to me. My new years resolution is to practice gratitude for my survival skills and to love myself through this process. My new years resolution is to take selfies, watch shows I like, and hang out with people who are patient and kind. My new years resolution is to keep growing, keep healing and at the same time be okay with where I am.

Here's to 2016, may it be a year of growth, but not shame.

Making Space for my Gender is Part of my Trauma Recovery

Trauma recovery is a whole process, a process of wholeness. I have found that the hardest thing about trauma recovery is it requires the skill of self advocacy which is a skill trauma survivors can have a hard time with (we are used to our voices not mattering). But asking for what we need, often over and over, often from many different sources, is essential to the work. For me, trying to get appropriate trauma care has become harder since coming out as nonbinary. Suddenly I am an inconvenience and over complicating things. I am throwing a wrench in simplistic narratives about violence against women. I am asking for a pronoun that many see as awkward or grammatically incorrect and I am asking for it from a body that isn't read as in need of another pronoun. But loving myself is the constant work of remembering and insisting that creating space for my gender is part of my process of trauma recovery. Being forced into a gender and sexual orientation that weren't mine is part of my trauma. And yet in this process of trying to self advocate and trying to heal it is important to remember that this pain and these traumas are not mine alone. I am not the only one who feels and experiences these things. There are pains too that are invisible to me because of my privileges and it is my responsibility to see them and to do the work of stopping my contributions to them. Trauma can be isolating when it feels like me against the world but it can also be a common ground and a way to come together. Part of the process of recovery is to stop thinking only of the survival of the self and to begin to think about the survival of all of us, to begin to see and make space for the complicated ways that we are implicated in each others traumas and the complicated ways that we are responsible for each others liberation.

Snapshots in Trauma Time

The social worker is driving me home from the police station. She says I did a good job. She says a lot of people get their stories mixed up. She says they can't tell it the same way twice.

I am lying in bed, terror gripping my entire being. Methodically I tell myself the story. Each detail. The sinking pedal boat. Swimming home to get my dad. Cutting my foot. Sending my dad after them. Bandaging my foot in the bathroom. My grandfather entering the room. I tell myself the story again. The context. The beginning. The middle. The end. I have the story. The memory itself, I don't know.

I say to my mom I was eleven when it happened. She tells me no, I was twelve. I argue with her. I was eleven. It was the summer after grade six. I am sure of it. She tells me details, the trip she was on when it happened, the year was 1999. I was twelve. I remember my bathing suit. The one I was wearing. Yellow, with white flowers.

I am running late for my class at the university. I am always running late. I scramble across campus and make it to the classroom door. I look through the little glass window. Who are those people in there? I don't recognize any of them. I check the time. Yes, it's the right time. I am only a little late. Hesitantly I enter. I look at them. They look at me. Something is wrong. These aren't the right people. I leave. I feel perplexed, disoriented. I am questioning my grip on reality. I pass a newspaper box and see the date. It is not the day I thought it was.

I tell this story to a therapist. I feel crazy sometimes, I say. I can't keep track of things. She tells me this is a common response to trauma. It's trauma related she says.

I am staring at a plastic cup of water. The room is cold. I feel sick. The jury is to my left. I don't look at them. He is to my right. I don't look at him. The defense lawyer asks me how long it lasted. I try to produce a number. The number references a void. I was not there when it happened. I know because I kept the story. The memory never formed.

Time slows down like we are under water. Each moment unfolds more like a ripple than a singular event. The impossibility of each action, the resistance against the inevitable outcome. He is angry again. I am caught in a storm. This is a moment I would replay if I could remember it. This is a moment I will be forced to reconstruct again and again, on camera, in front of a jury.

This is a moment that isn't happening. This is an impossible moment. The blow of impacts are softened by the lack of memory. The bruises and the pictures tell a story. The body does not experience what cannot happen. What could not have happened has.

Never Enough: Alcoholic at Sixteen, Sober at Twenty-five

(This piece appeared on shedoesthecity.com)

My first drink was a shot of vodka with a little bit of sugar in it. I was sixteen years old and hanging out with some older teenagers and twenty-somethings. They thought it was adorable that I'd never had a drink and immediately got me drinking. My memory of that night comes in pieces: chugging red wine from the bottle over a sink and chasing it with a litre of Pepsi, the wine bottle smashing as I tried to prevent them from taking it from me, crying and talking at length about my abuse-filled childhood, making out with this girl while her boyfriend was in the other room, him walking in and a dramatic break up ensuing. I was still drunk in the morning as everyone lay passed out around the house. I had, from anyone's perspective but mine, caused a number of huge scenes and embarrassed myself. From my perspective, I had just had the best night of my life. I felt *good,* which, for a chronically depressed and traumatized teenager, was an incredibly rare thing.

The second time I drank, I was hit with a wave of depression. This was nothing new, but what was new was the clarity and courage that the alcohol brought to the depression. I had been suicidal for years and had made a few halfhearted suicide attempts, but I never had the courage to really act on it. There, drunk in my room, with my best friend sprawled out on the floor (we were pre-drinking before a party we never got to), it suddenly seemed so easy. I drunkenly found a bottle of Advil and, without my friend's knowledge, began swallowing the pills one at a time. It was only when I reached into the bottle and found it empty that I realized what I had done. I was suddenly gripped with fear. Drunk out of my mind, I started trying to puke up the pills but couldn't get them up. For some reason I thought it would be a good idea to drink shampoo, believing this would induce vomiting. Instead, it burned and I was choking up bubbly bile without being able to get the pills up. My friend managed to get me to a hospital where I drank charcoal and was formed.

The third time I drank I was at a large party. Having consumed all the drinks I had, I went around taking other people's drinks. Being seventeen, inexperienced, naive, and incredibly drunk, I didn't realize that hard liquor was somewhat different from the coolers I had been drinking. I took a twenty-sixer of hard liquor out of someone's hands, tipped it back and chugged. I drank the entire thing. I went into a blackout, of which I remember only slivers. I was considered a danger to myself and others. I was taken in ambulance with a police escort to a hospital. I was admitted to the psych ward and remained drunk for days. My blood alcohol level was about eight times what is legally considered 'drunk.' The doctors said it was a miracle I wasn't in a coma. When I sobered up enough to stop screaming, a group of doctors and my parents sat me down. The doctors told me that it seemed like I had a problem with alcohol. I thought this was ridiculous. I had been drunk three times. There was no way that a person who had only been drunk three times could be an alcoholic. I admitted that I had mental health issues, and that this was interacting badly with the alcohol, but that did not mean I had an alcohol problem.

I continued to drink. Mental health episodes were common. Blacking out was usual. Hangovers that left me sick, puking, and shaking for an entire day were standard. I had a difficult time maintaining friendships, or any other interests in my life. The only people I wanted to hang out with were people who drank like I drank, people who drank to get wasted. Even then, I always nervously eyed the alcohol supply, watching how much they were drinking, how much I was drinking, and worrying that there wouldn't be enough. The truth is there was never enough. No matter how drunk I got, I always wanted more. No matter how many scenes I caused, or how sick I got, drinking never seemed like a bad idea.

At the age of twenty-four I decided to take a break from drinking. I had tried many times in the past and had never lasted more than a few days. This time my motivation was to save a relationship, and I tried harder than I ever had before. I continued smoking weed from morning to night (another habit I had picked up along the way) but I didn't drink. After a few months off the alcohol, I decided to stay away from alcohol for an entire year. During this year an amazing thing happened. I made friends. My life started to blossom. Because I wasn't getting drunk, causing scenes, and saying all sorts of regrettable things, I was able to maintain friendships for the first time since I started drinking. I was still under a fog of marijuana smoke and spending more money on weed than on rent, but my life had drastically improved. I no longer found myself in strange places, on park benches, in ambulances, or in strangers' apartments. I actually had people in my life who thought I was an okay person.

The friends I made drank. I would often hang out with them while they were drinking. They drank a lot, but they didn't seem as crazy as me. They didn't end up on park benches or in ambulances, but they did frequently end up in strangers' apartments. Binge drinking was normal, and since they didn't cause as many scenes as I did, their drinking seemed a lot more manageable. They were what I aspired to be. Twenty-something year olds who got drunk on the weekends and had fun, who acted crazy but not too crazy. Not drinking started to become harder and harder. I felt like the odd one out. I watched them all laughing and having fun. I tried to be a part of it while feeling awkward and self-conscious, yet I stayed true to my decision not to drink for one year. I needed to prove to myself that I could. I believed that if I could stay alcohol-free for one year I would no longer be an alcoholic. I believed that if I could say no to all drinks for one year, I would then be able to say no to sixth drink, or wherever was a normal place to stop.

When my one year arrived, I waited a day or two because I didn't want to seem too eager. Then, as casually as I could, trying to hide my incredible eagerness, I announced to my friends that I would join them in drinking. They were all overjoyed and excited to have me. That first night of drinking, I got drunk. I don't know how many drinks I had but I didn't stop at any point. I went home with a random guy and was wandering back from his place at 5am, still drunk. This felt like a success. There were no ambulances, no scenes, just the regular behaviour of binge drinking. I was back, and I was convinced I was no longer an alcoholic. I joined my friends in their pre-drinking and bar hopping, in their summer days on the balcony drinking nonstop, in their occasional crying or arguments, and mine. It all seemed normal and fun and what everyone else in their twenties was doing. I was glad to have left the dysfunctional drinking of my past behind me.

Within three months I had destroyed every relationship I had built in my year of not drinking. I screamed at people. I said awful things. I was mean and inconsiderate, and only cared about drinking. Within three months of that hopeful first drink, I was out in a valley I had drunkenly wandered into. I had lost my shoes and stepped on glass, and I was bleeding everywhere. You would think it would seem obvious that my experiment of attempting to be a social drinker had failed. You would think that I would immediately put down the booze, apologize, and straighten out my life. But I couldn't. Despite the chaos, the pain, the loneliness, the embarrassment, I loved drinking. I needed drinking. I didn't want to stop.

Fast forward a little less than another year and I was still going strong. My blackouts became more and more frequent. One minute I was in a bar, and the next thing I knew I was naked in some strange bed and there was a man yelling at me, calling me a crazy bitch, and telling me to get out of his apartment. I didn't know who he was, where I was, or why he was calling me a crazy bitch, but I could assume from the context that we had sex, sex that I did not remember at all, and I could not say whether or not we had used protection. My life was lonely, small, and scary, like it had been since I started drinking. Part of me wanted to try to stop again, but a life without drinking honestly didn't seem like a life worth living.

Through a twist of fate, an old friend I hadn't spoken to in years got in touch and asked me to go to lunch. She brought along another friend of hers. During this lunch date I brought up that I was thinking of taking another break from drinking. The friend of my old friend handed me a piece of paper with the names of some meetings written on it. She explained that she attended twelve-step meetings and that this was how she stayed sober. I was skeptical, but I was also desperate. I decided that I would check out a meeting.

When I got to the meeting I heard people describing something which I lived but which I had never been able to explain. They didn't all have the same experiences as me, or drink in the exact same way that I did, but they understood the underlying feelings. They were describing the experience of going back to drinking, over and over again, despite the severe consequences. They were talking about how limits like "I will only have six" or "I will only buy three so I will only drink three" fell away completely once they started to drink. They were saying out loud what I was too afraid to say: that despite the horrific consequences of alcoholic drinking, the alternative seemed worse. A life without alcohol did not seem like a life worth living.

But they were also saying other things. Some were talking about how they used to feel this way, but that they now had full, fulfilling lives, and five, ten, twenty years of sobriety. They were talking about how they stayed sober and why they were grateful for their sobriety. For the first time, I felt a flicker of hope. I decided to come back, and I kept coming back.

I am now coming up on four years of sobriety, which to me means complete abstinence from drugs and alcohol. I have friends, community, and a loving partner. I am in school studying what I am passionate about. I remember what I did last night and I no longer spend days on the floor in front of the toilet. Most importantly, I love myself. Sobriety has utterly transformed my life. It has opened up doorways, which I wouldn't have believed possible. At the same time, the journey has just begun and I am learning more every day. I am incredibly grateful for my sobriety. When I look back at my life before, it is unbelievable to me that I spent so many years feeling lonely, unsafe, hurting myself and others, and being completely powerless to stop.

I am an alcoholic. This means that I cannot safely drink. It means that once I put alcohol into my body I lose all ability to control how much I will drink, what I will do, or what will happen to me. It means that I need to prioritize sobriety as the centre of my life, as the foundation on which the rest of my life is built. It means that I need the help, support, and solidarity of other alcoholics on this journey.

My sobriety does not mean that I judge the person I used to be, or others who are in that position. Just the opposite. I have profound compassion and empathy for everyone who struggles with addiction, including myself. I hope that everyone is able to be supported in the way that they need to be supported. I believe that everyone should have access to health care and community support that works for them. I believe in harm reduction as a spectrum that can include support for complete abstinence (which is what I need) and also things like support for using certain substances and not others, support for finding ways to moderate, access to clean injection supplies and pipes, access to safer sex supplies, and communities that support and respect our different and complicated relationships to substance use. I believe in cross solidarity among sober alcoholics/addicts, active alcoholics/addicts, and drug users. I believe in the decriminalization of all drugs, and I long for a culture that helps people rather than punishes them.

Sobriety is what I need, and I want support for getting sober to be available to everyone who needs and wants it. I want to see a cultural shift in which there are alternative social events that do not centre on drinking. I want to see a cultural shift where young people struggling with addiction don't fear seeking the help they need, believing that sobriety will be a social death sentence. I share my story because I want people to know that it is possible. It is possible to be an alcoholic at sixteen years old. It is possible to get sober, and stay sober, at twenty-five (and I know people who got sober, and stayed sober, at fifteen, nineteen, twenty). It is possible to have a rich, full, and satisfying life without drinking. And if you are struggling, you are not alone.

Voicemail

Don't claim to love me if you haven't spoken to me in fifteen years, if you watched your husband sexualize me my entire childhood, if you took my pictures down when I told the truth and erased me from existence, don't claim to love me now, don't call me on my phone, on a number I never gave you, and tell my voicemail that you love me. You don't know me. The last you saw me I was a child who desperately needed your help. Now I'm an adult, and I have built an entire life for myself, working against the current of an unrelenting trauma, the legacy of growing up in a house of sexual abuse. And I have felt guilty for years because I thought I abandoned you, betrayed you, for simply stating the truth. But it was you who abandoned and betrayed me. Love is not a word. Love is an action, and you have not shown me one action of love.

Nonbinary Pasts, Nonbinary Futures

My pronouns are they/them. I didn't know this until I was in my late twenties. I was coercively gendered female my entire life. By my teens I knew that wasn't the whole picture, but my love for femme made me unsure of where I could possibly fit under the trans umbrella. Finding my way to nonbinary took time.

But my nonbinary is time traveling. I like to reach back into the past and grant the little kid I was the freedom not to be a girl. Just because I used to go by 'she' does not mean that you can apply 'she' to me when talking about me in the past. If I decide, for myself, that I want to explore an aspect of myself under the pronoun 'she', that doesn't mean that you can. If I tell you my pronouns are they/them, you should be using them, for the past, for the future, unless or until I tell you otherwise.

I like to reach into the future and grant myself permission to be an aging or elderly femme human without having to be lumped into the category 'woman' in order to exist. I am interested in nonbinary temporalities, arriving in a nonbinary present, which could be any moment in time.

Resist temptation to remember me as a girl or to imagine me as a woman. Imagine femme futurity in all its brilliance. Imagine a world where 'they' pronouns no longer cause confusion. Imagine nonbinary futures traveling back in time to reach us and catch us up to speed.

Want

I want to cut off my hair. I want to feel my body again. I want to be somewhere, by a lake, in a field, where I could remove my clothes and lie on the ground, jump in the water. I want to wander down alleyways again, looking for all the secret places which we take for granted. I want to trust my ear. I want to trust my hands. I want to trust my word. I want to trust myself again.

I know that I am more than one person. Right now the ache of old pain is making me want to crack open. I can't, I don't want to be anything other than what I am. I feel this urgency, this pull. It's not nothingness that's calling me, it's something else. I want to be free. I want to move through time and space. I want to forgive myself.

I'm doing the best I can and I've gotten this far. But I am still carrying a weight I should not be carrying. It slows me down and makes me sluggish. Makes me tired and disoriented. Makes me not trust myself. I want to be able to say the truth. I don't want to have to hold the truth, all alone, anymore.

The words *I believe you* are not enough. I want you to know.

Queering Condoms

Putting a condom on a penis does not have to mean that penetrative sex is about to happen. Putting a condom on a penis might mean a desire for closeness, contact, without worry about fluids. Putting a condom on a penis might mean grinding, rubbing, touching. It might mean rolling around naked, body parts all over the place. It does not mean adherence to a heteronormative script of 'foreplay is over and now we are fucking'... we are already fucking, there is no foreplay, just play. We are good. In, on, around, whatever, but it is up to us, not some pre-determined script. We get to decide the time line, the actions, what feels good to us. Condoms can go on and come off without climax, depending on what actions are happening a condom might be wanted or might not. Condoms can be about personal boundaries, care, freeing the mind of worry. They can mean lots of things. And they don't have to mean penetrative sex.

Frozen // River Veins

My body doesn't move, becomes frozen, ceases. This freezing has its precise moments. Words like stones unsayable. Limbs heavy connected to spirit with a thin thread, being dragged along until the body can be put somewhere safe.

But this freezing also spreads into other moments. Moments not marked as especially anything. This freezing takes the shape of a hesitancy, a slowness, a sluggishness, a self-consciousness. My body is a map of pain. My body is a constellation of violations. My body is a map of shame.

don'ttouchmedon'ttouchmedon'tfuckingtouchme

The ultrasound technician is tracing my veins. I had no idea these rivers existed within me, deep, and hidden. Tiny, invisible veins which are also a network of rivers, their own ecosystems. His fingers slip under the edge of my underwear, because this is where the veins go. I had no idea this would be 'so invasive'. My eyes are projected at a ceiling like all the ceilings I have ever seen. I am well aware of not being. I am frozen, not moving, not here.

I think about the rivers of my veins, existing under the surface of my frozen body, like currents still moving under ice.

I Shaved My Head Because...

Because I always believed I was ugly, that somehow the long hair covered that up, maybe even transformed it into beauty. Because when I was a kid I was called moon face or the less flattering man head and told that my head was too big for my body. Because I believed that somehow my long hair drew attention away from my rosacea. Because I was exhausted. Because being good is exhausting. Because being desirable, attractive, pretty, fuckable, but not too slutty, but not too vain, is exhausting. Because my father loved my hair. Because he was mad when I dyed it purple at the age of thirteen. Because I have been bleaching and dying my hair for sixteen years. Because I have psoriasis all over my scalp, like I used to have all over my body. Because I wanted to grieve, I needed to sever. Because I was done. Because I couldn't be afraid anymore. Because I needed to purge, release, be free. Because I didn't want to have to try to be something I'm not anymore. Because I wanted to run water over my head or go swimming without worrying how long it would take my hair to dry or how much the dye would fade. Because of my genders. Because of my masculinity, which is begging to be reborn. Because of my femme-ininity, which seeks freedom from cages. Because I am nonbinary. Because my gender dysphoria is very hard to explain. Because my gender euphoria makes my dick hard and my heart soft and my eyes glow. Because I am a witch, a healer, and this was the healing I needed. Because I lit the candle and lay down the cards: Death, The High Priestess, The Fool, and I was ready. Because I am an incest survivor and my body has never been my own. Because I am an incest survivor and my body has never been my own. Because I am an incest survivor and my body has never been my own. Because I wanted courage, I wanted freedom. Because I wanted to be inside this body, not outside looking at it. Because it was time. Because when I was sixteen I gave myself a chelsea even though I wanted to shave the whole thing, because I didn't think I could pull off the whole thing. Because my rapist boyfriend was not happy that I gave myself a chelsea. Because I got called names and I just grew my hair out because I was convinced they were right and I was ugly. Because I want to feel my skull in my hands. Because I want to feel the heat and power of my being. Because it is not my responsibility to be anything other than what I am. Because I wanted to.

Shipping: Healing Sexual Trauma and Discovering What Turns Me On

Ever since I was a little kid I got off by fantasizing about rape and abusive power dynamics. I was introduced to sexuality through childhood sexual abuse followed soon after by the discovery of porn and random men on the internet and my brain wired in such a way that I got off on abusive stuff. As I got older I tried to reclaim this by being submissive in bed in BDSM contexts and also just generally. I couldn't get off any other way. I don't think there's anything wrong with these types of fantasies or with power play or BDSM. But I never had a choice. I never had the opportunity to find out what would turn me on outside of violence. Lately in my recovery I have taken a break from sex and have started trying to explore fantasies in a different way. I can now completely get off on these romantic plots in random TV shows. I am so proud of myself. Like I can actually experience sexuality that isn't about violence and I don't feel dissociative and awful after. I feel weird admitting that romantic shipping youtube videos are pretty much my porn. And like, I feel it would be way more acceptable to say I like actual porn or whatever. But my truth is that I am a romantic. My turn ons are connection and being cared for. I get off on the idea of two people in love. This truth is hard won for me. And I feel like women and feminine people are shamed and stereotyped for 'wanting romance' and we are expected to 'be chill' and be down to fuck and to 'not be like the other girls' and 'not need a relationship' or whatever. I did that shit for years. And it would be fine if that's what I really wanted. But it was all a lie. I wanted sweetness and kindness and care and love but I didn't think I could possibly get it so I settled for three am texts. Like honestly I am so proud of myself for admitting that I am into romance and feelings and love and connection and that I deserve those things.

Survivors for Prison Abolition

Courts don't own the truth. Cops don't own the truth. I have been failed by police and courts every step of the way. They have inserted themselves into my life, said they would protect me, re-traumatized me, and failed me. I realize it is my whiteness that even allowed me to believe they might help me. They didn't. And they actively harm survivors of colour all the time, pressing charges on racialized women who report intimate partner violence. A guilty verdict is not a success or victory. A not guilty verdict does not mean that what happened didn't happen. It happened. The survivors are telling the truth. As communities we need to find ways to support survivors and address sexual and gendered violence in our communities. And a big part of this is taking the authority away from cops and courts and deciding to believe and protect each other. I want movements for survivors of sexual and gendered violence to push for prison abolition, not reform.

Grad School Life

Grad school has been sucking up all my time. So much reading, so many papers. I am really enjoying it. It is also hard. Hard to navigate academia in my disabled traumatized bodymind. Hard to do the work and be okay at the same time. Hard to have time to do anything else.

My research is about trauma as a way of being in the world, as a call for justice, as potentiality for strange resonances and intimacies. My research is about queer temporalities and nonhuman beings and ecological ethics and trauma as a way of being. My research is about world-making and transformation rooted in disabled embodiment. I actually love what I am learning, thinking, writing and exploring.

There is so much more that I want to be reading and I feel like there is never enough time for everything. I am also, somehow, in the midst of all of this, trying to maintain a commitment to my creative work, trying to keep my creative work and my academic work in conversation and informed by one another. I haven't made a zine in a few months. But I am writing this now.

I want and need to resist the inherent ableism of academia. I want and need to make apparent the important work and knowledge production of marginalized communities who are simultaneously sucked up into and erased by academia. I want and need to resist academia while existing within it.

Part of how I do this is by sharing my work, ideas, and process openly on the internet. Part of how I do this is citing lived experience, zines, poetry, blogs, and various forms of knowledge production, alongside academic texts. Part of how I do this is by constantly learning and unlearning inside and outside of the classroom. Part of how I do this is being honest about it all.

Accessing Health Care Should Not Equal Incarceration

Recently I needed to go to the emergency room. At the hospital the nurse was asking me if I've had any alcohol or drugs recently. And I was like "No, I'm sober." And the nurse was like "When was the last time you had a drink?" Perhaps thinking I meant I was sober that very moment. I replied "2012." The nurse gave me a knowing look and said "Congratulations."

I used to escape from hospitals when I ended up there because I knew they wouldn't let me leave. I have been formed and locked up multiple times. It's such a different experience accessing health care in sobriety. Like I am not afraid they won't let me leave. The power and freedom of that. There's still the regular bullshit of hospitals but I don't feel I am being looked at with condescension, disgust, or blame. The health care system needs to do better in the way they treat people who end up in emergency drunk or high. Like I have had so many concussions, needed stitches, overdosed and had massive alcohol poisoning without any medical attention because I was too scared to access it.

Health care should not equal incarceration. Period.

Holding Complexity: Compulsive Sexuality and Trauma

I need a way to talk about compulsive sexuality. I need a way to tell my story. I need a way for my story to be heard. I need a way to say these things without the narratives that are imposed upon me. Without being called a disgusting slut AND without over simplistic celebratory narratives of empowered sexuality. I need space for my complexity. For the complexity of being an incest survivor. For the complexity of dense, layered trauma. For the complexity of the choices we make when we don't really have choices. I never had a choice about sex. Sexuality was imposed upon me as a child, in my family, and as I grew older, and got out into the world, I was assaulted and raped again and again. Because I had no tools for how to stop it. Because I had no idea I had a choice.

And then I became a slut. I fucked random guys who I met on the street. I fucked groups of guys one after the other. I fucked for money and for free. I fucked outside and in strange empty condos and in warehouses and on bathroom floors. I fucked strangers, regularly. I sucked dick and got cum on my face and I cheated on all my boyfriends and I had sex with married men. I liked it, loved it, needed it, was obsessed with it, hated it, was traumatized by it, all at once. I was nothing to most of these guys. They treated me like I was completely disposable. I pretended I didn't care but I would frequently throw drunken fits. Because I wanted to be cared about, I just had no idea how.

And then, when I did fall in love and start a monogamous relationship, my partner called me a disgusting slut who was 'running my pussy all over town'. He went into great, explicit detail about how fucking disgusting he thought I was, how I was so lucky he was even with me, because no other man would ever want to be with a disgusting slut like me. And even though he twisted my limbs, bent my fingers back, screamed at me, flipped the furniture in the house, kicked me in the stomach, put me through the wall, he maintained that I was lucky to have him, that he was the best that I would ever get.

Those words still ring in my ears and I feel defensive about my promiscuous days. I have latched on to narratives of empowerment. I wrote a widely circulated piece called 'yes i am a slut'. I wanted to find a way to feel good about my past, to silence the hateful words that were thrown at me, to show that there is nothing wrong with all the fucking that I did. And there is nothing wrong with it. There is nothing shameful about it. There is nothing about it that makes me unworthy of love or deserving of violence. There is nothing wrong with having sex with strangers, or in strange places, or for money, or with groups of guys one after the other. There is nothing wrong with it AND I need a way to talk about this that honours the complexity of my truth.

And my truth is that it was painful. It was pleasurable and it was painful. It was compulsive and it was awful. A lot of it I was way too drunk to truly consent to. A lot of it was with guys who were mean and disrespectful to me. And, all of it was in the context of me being an incest survivor, of me never having a choice not to be sexual, of me making the best of a bad situation, of me finding a way to enjoy something that I felt there was no way not to do. The complexity of the compulsive sexuality trauma brain is something that so few people understand. And I hate the over-simplistic narratives: either I'm a disgusting slut, a tragedy, or a super empowered sexual being. None of that is accurate. All of it is way more complex, and even I don't have the words for it yet.

I want there to be space to honour the wisdom of sucking dick, of having sex in a university class room and not getting caught, of drunkenly screaming at a guy for fucking me but refusing to kiss me because I am a 'slut'. I want there to be space to honour the wisdom of the way I survived, the way I found what pleasure I could, the way I tried to make sense of the sexual violence that was and is my reality. I want there to be room for the wisdom of being honest about pain, denying pain, pretending it's better than it is, fucking in cheap motel rooms, going into the bathroom to cry, cheating on boyfriends, being the 'other woman', being the trash that everyone fucks but no one loves. I want space for the wisdom and the healing that comes from moving through all of this and owning it and not seeking simple answers but wanting the complexity to just be.

I need a way to talk about this, without shame, without hollow celebration, with honesty, and courage, and respect. I need a way to move past the narratives and stereotypes that have been forced upon me and to tell my own truth. I need a way to talk about the pain without being called 'sex negative'. I need a way to talk about the pleasure without being called disgusting. I need to find the words to speak about compulsive sexuality, without shame, without condemnation, without simplification. I need a way to tell my truth and to be heard and to be honoured and witnessed and held. There is incredible wisdom that I have gained through these experiences. There is incredible pain that I have endured. There is incredible healing that I have found in being honest, in the face of shaming and silencing and violence, being honest anyway and insisting on my truth. It is complicated. Trauma is complicated. And the ways that I have survived, are the ways that I have survived.

Capitalism Hurts Our Creative Power

We are put in competition with each other. We sell out the heart of our work in order to make it more consumable. We are taught to regard other artists (who are our teachers and fellow travelers) with suspicion and jealousy. We retreat inward, sometimes discovering the gems we are holding inside, sometimes in hiding from the rest of the world. Capitalism hurts our creative power. We need to find a way to work under these conditions. We need to survive in this climate and we need to make the art that we are here to make. An important part of that is working to heal relationships, with self, with community, with fellow artists, with creativity itself, in the spirit of generosity, honesty, and kindness. Do the work you are here to do. Support other artists with all of your heart.

Traumatized Extrovert, Learned Introvert

I think I am a traumatized extrovert, a learned introvert. Because I do love to talk. I do love to jump in. I do love to engage and share myself outwardly. I just get overstimulated and overwhelmed. I get stressed out. The reason for this is fear, it's the circling in my head, the worrying. Worrying about every single dynamic. Scanning, constantly scanning for threats. Thinking that people don't like me, or that they are judging me, stressing for saying or doing something I wish I hadn't. Imagine the feeling of just being. Of just being present, in the moment, without this parade of terror and stress and anxiety running through my mind and body.

I wasn't always this way. As a kid I was extremely outgoing, a chatterbox they called me. Always telling stories, jumping in, volunteering, raising my hand, wanting to take part. This slowly was taken away. I became more and more introverted, withdrawn, sullen, as I became more and more traumatized. I learned that the world was not a safe place and became extremely hypervigilant, agonizing over every little thing.

That's what drinking does: it takes the edge off. It makes that cacophony disappear. It makes me relax. It makes me at ease. It makes everything okay. Or, there were brief moments where I felt that way. Then it became about chasing that feeling, desperately hunting it down, desperately trying to guard against its loss, desperately trying to recreate it. And not being able to. And not being able to stop. And creating situations which amplified the existing feeling of being unsafe and unwanted. The drinking stopped working but I kept drinking. The stress of simply being with others was, and is, way too much for me to deal with.

In sobriety, when I am spiritually connected, I have had moments of experiencing that ease. But I fall too easily back into the stress, and shame, and terror. I climb out and I fall back. I fall back most easily when I am with other people, especially in groups. In groups there are so many dynamics, so many potential stressors, so many things for me to read into, and get hung up on. It saps up all my energy and I feel sick and exhausted. So, I call myself an introvert. It is so much easier for me to feel spiritually connected, and therefore at ease, at peace, when I am alone.

When it is me and my bike, me and the moon, me and the squirrels and the birds and the trees. When it is me and a book, me and a room full of strangers who I am not expected to interact with, me and the night. I remember my connection to the universe. I remember my inherent, irrevocable worthiness and right to be here. I feel alive. I feel safe. I feel a much more rooted, much more steady, much more vivid version of the feeling which I sought in the bottle, over and over again.

Why do people stress me out so much? Why do I feel so terrified, overwhelmed, anxious? Why do I feel deeply unworthy? Why do I feel so completely drained after engaging in a group? Why do I prefer my own company? Why do I isolate? All of this is connected, and all roads lead to the same place: trauma. Repetitive experiences of violence and neglect, starting in childhood.

Human beings were the source of my trauma. Navigating family dynamics in a dysfunctional family, attempting to shield myself from further harm, hoping to find a way to win safety, these things produce hypervigilance. And hypervigilance in the context of complex trauma in not just fear of being assaulted again. It's not just looking behind your shower curtain, or double checking the door is locked, or being startled by loud noises.

The hypervigilance of complex trauma is embedded in everyday interactions, in relationships, because this is where the trauma started. The hypervigilance of complex trauma means that criticism (perceived or real) can be experienced as an actual threat to safety. It means that feeling like you said or did something you wish you hadn't can result in immobilizing, relentless shame. It means that every action taken and sentence spoken by another person can be viewed with suspicion, constantly seeking out the threat. It means feeling unwelcome, unwanted, and deeply unsafe, in regular, everyday interactions.

So, of course, social interactions can be incredibly stressful and exhausting. It makes sense that they would overwhelm me and that I would pull away. It makes sense that I would isolate and hide behind the title 'introvert'. There are a ton of clickbait articles circling on the internet which present introversion as a legitimate and valuable personality type, and it certainly is. But rarely do we look any deeper than that. Rarely to we consider that the 'introverted' adult who feels completely done in by an hour of hanging out in a group might have been a loud, rambunctious child at one point. Rarely do we consider that some 'introverts' are actually experiencing very severe trauma symptoms and calling it introversion to be legible and to not bring up a difficult topic.

I am realizing that I may not be an introvert after all. That loud, talkative, spontaneous child still exists within me. And with the right care, and continued recovery and healing, I hope to create space in which to safely explore that aspect of who I am. In the meantime, I would like a trauma and disability analysis to enter into conversations on introversion, and for us as communities to be gentle with each other because many of us are carrying a lot of pain.

Quitting Coffee and Social Media

I'm an addict, which means I engage in compulsive behaviours to escape pain. I have a lot of pain, physical and emotional and not easily divided into that binary. I experience a lot of pain because I have experienced a lot of violence and because I experienced abandonment as a child.

I have been sober for over four years. I have accomplished this through twelve step programs, spirituality, willingness, and surrender. I have accomplished this by putting my recovery first. I have reached a new chapter in my recovery. I recently joined another fellowship, one which uses the twelve steps to address childhood trauma. I found this fellowship because it is time. I am at a place where old habits are no longer serving me. I am being called to go deeper, to heal deeper, to surrender at a deeper level, to change.

Recently it occurred to me how much money I was spending on coffee. A lot. I was drinking a soy latte every day. I like my coffee really creamy and ever since going vegan I was really unsatisfied with the watery soy milk in my coffee so I started drinking lattes. At first as a treat, then every day. I had been drinking coffee every day for a long time, and now the habit was becoming even more expensive. As a person living on disability it was pretty ridiculous how much I was spending but I justified it.

What prompted me to change was when I realized I got a withdrawal headache if I didn't have a coffee. As a person who gets chronic migraines I can't afford a withdrawal headache. If it becomes a migraine it can really cost me a lot. So I made a decision and I started to ween myself off with black tea. I'm not totally caffeine free, as I will have the occasional green or black tea. But I've been coffee free for over a month now.

The next change was even bigger. Anyone who knows me know that I'm always on Facebook. And instagram. And sometimes twitter and tumblr. I'm obsessed, actually, addicted to social media. It was a total compulsion. I was on my phone first thing in the morning, and for hours every day. I would try to set limits for myself by deleting apps off my phone, or setting time limits, but I never followed these. I always ended up re-downloading the app, and going over my limit.

I had really mixed feelings about giving up social media. As an anxious, stressed out, trauma human, social media, especially Facebook, was my primary means of connecting with people. It was my main access point to community. At the same time, I realized that while it kept me connected, it did so in a superficial way. I had a ton of acquaintances and friends I didn't know well, but not a lot of close friendships.

I struggle so much with building friendships and intimacy because of my C-PTSD/trauma/child abuse stuff, and I wanted to believe that social media was helping, that it was better than nothing. And, in many ways, that was true. At the same time, it allowed me to feel like I had connection, but at the end of the day, I still felt desperately lonely and didn't know how to connect with people on a deeper level.

On top of this, Facebook was flaring up my jealousy, and jealousy is one of my biggest, if not my biggest, mental health trigger. Mostly I was jealous of other people's friendships with each other, as I felt like an outsider, unable to have close relationships.

My compulsive use of Facebook was an attempt to escape pain, and it started making the pain worse, which, in my experience, is the typical evolution of addiction. First it seems to help, then it makes the pain worse, so I use it more to try to feel better again, but it has stopped working.

I had been toying with the idea of deleting social media for months but I always talked myself out of it. I always listed off what I loved about it and told myself I could make it work. But finally, I hit a rock bottom. All the trauma stuff has been coming up and I have been getting honest about my compulsions, and I have finally found the willingness to surrender and try something new.

After letting people know what I was going to do I deactivated my Facebook and deleted all social media apps on my phone. The only things I'm allowing are goodreads, duolingo, and wordpress. So you can still find me there. Otherwise, I'm off social media.

It's been a few weeks. The first day or two were extremely uncomfortable. I was in a lot of pain and I didn't have my compulsion to medicate it. Fear, anxiety, worry, depression, sadness, stress, intrusive thoughts, you know, the usual. I'm being gentle with myself.

Even though it's been hard, I feel really good about my decision. I have decided to get back to basics and put my recovery first. I have decided to surrender compulsive behaviours whenever and wherever I can. I have decided to feel the sadness and the pain, and to try to find a way to grieve. I have decided to buy a journal and start writing again instead of posting every thought I have on Facebook.

It's a huge change in my life, but as I sit here listening to the wind in the trees, feeling cool air come in through my window, I know that I am moving closer to my truth, to my connection to the universe, to my healing. I know that the journey is ongoing, and more will be revealed.

Waking Up

I quit coffee. I quit social media. I took out all my facial piercings. I'm seeing a naturopath. I'm learning about my ancestors. I planted Joe Pyeweed, Bee Balm, Woodland Sunflower, Columbine, Swamp Milkweed, two types of Coneflower, and a Blackberry Bush, in the hopes of helping the Rusty Patched Bumblebee. In the morning I go out into the garden barefoot and check on the plants. I water them with a watering can. I joined the gym. I work out on the machines or go to classes. It feels really good to move my body. I ride my bike everywhere. I got new tires because I kept getting flats. I am active in two 12 step programs. I have a sponsor and I'm working the steps in both. It's a lot of work. Recovery is a full time job but then there's still school work and other stuff to do. Feelings are rising to the surface. Denial is cracking open. I am seeing what is underneath. I am brewing Holy Basil tea in a large glass jar, drinking it all day. I am drawing cards at my altar and writing in a journal. I am wearing sunscreen and sunglasses and a helmet when I ride my bike. I am reading multiple books at once. I am beginning to remember my place in the universe, that I am part of this universe. I am waking up. But at the same time, I am still struggling. Depression is deep and trauma is complex. Magic abounds. Each action, a spell. Creating a craft. Setting intentions. Believing. Manifesting. Diving. Divining. The magic is action. Practice. The magic is also letting go. Surrender.

Questions

I am in process right now. I am in liminal space. I have lost all sense of certainty but I have developed a sense of faith. It makes me feel like I don't know what to write. I write in my diary every day. The words come easily. But here, in a zine, the words I will share with others, I'm not sure what to write. I am becoming and unbecoming. I am transforming. This is what I have wanted and needed. A deep level of change. It is happening exactly as it should, exactly in its time. I am being transformed.

I am reading books. Lots of them. I am thinking about things. I am spending my time pondering, without coming to conclusions. I am asking the questions. One of my sponsors told me, *Write the questions down. Don't worry about the answers. Just write the questions.* I still haven't. Maybe because I don't know what the questions are, but more likely because I have been afraid.

What will happen when I start to write down the questions? What would change if the question became more important than the answer? What would change if the process became more important than the end result? Who would I be if I stopped being who I've been? What would happen if I said I didn't know? What would happen if I was wrong? What would happen if I took a risk? Can I still be safe if I let go of control? Can I trust the process? Who am I becoming? Where am I going? What will I lose? How painful will the loss be? Will I be able to hand the pain? Will I be able to grieve? What will be revealed? What will be made possible? What are my assumptions? What don't I know?

What inspires me? What am I grateful for? What excites me? What turns me on? What would happen if I asked for what I want? What if what I want changes? What if I don't know what I want? Is it okay not to know? Is it okay to change my mind? What will happen if I am criticized? What will happen if I am rejected? What will that feel like? What if the pain is disproportionate to what is going on? What if the pain is overwhelming? What if I use it to cement old patterns and beliefs? What if I use it as a foundation for change, for transformation?

How can I remember the magic all around me? How can I re-enchant the universe? How can I remember the truth in my DNA? How can I remember the magic? What would happen if I started to pay attention to the moon again? What would happen if I paid attention to the trees and found out their names? What would happen if I started listening for the birdsong, intentionally, consistently? What if I remembered my divinity? What if I remembered the sacred in all things?

What would happen if I asked for help? What would happen if I surrendered control? What would happen if I were truly willing to change? What would happen if I admitted that I don't know?

Reclaiming Bisexuality

When I was a kid I knew I was queer. I was in love with my female best friend for ten years. In grade five, during sex ed, we watched a video which described what a crush felt like. I was flooded with recognition because they were describing what I felt for my best friend. But then they said "these are perfectly normal feelings to have toward the opposite sex." I remember the feeling of dread that came over me. It clicked into place. I was not normal. From that point on, secretly, I identified as gay.

Then I would occasionally develop crushes on guys and I would be like "I guess I'm not gay after all" and I would push my very obvious queerness down. Then attraction toward women would come up again and I'd be like "okay I guess I am gay after all." I don't know when I first heard the term 'bisexual', but I didn't like it. It made me feel sick actually, because the word 'sexual' was right there, clear as day. As a child, and then teenager, who was surviving incestuous sexual violence, I saw sexuality as shameful, terrifying, and out of control. I didn't want to be sexual at all. And I certainly didn't want a sexual orientation that included the word 'sexual' right in it. I thought gay or straight sounded better. I knew, obviously, that straight was best of all. But gay at least hid the sexual aspect. It seemed more like an identity than an outright perversion. (This is not to dismiss the very real violence of homophobia, which I experienced firsthand when I came out as gay. This is just what I was thinking as a 13 – 14 year old and grappling with the concept of bisexuality.)

I came out as gay at 14 and dated my first girlfriend. This was in 2001, in a smalltown. I experienced a huge amount of homophobia, being called a dyke every day, being told I was disgusting and going to burn in hell, etc. But I didn't care because coming out had meant that a girl I had a crush on approached me and expressed interest, and honestly, I couldn't have been happier. Unfortunately, she broke my heart, cheated on me, left me and left the school. Leaving me the only dyke. I ended up developing a huge crush on a guy and then we started dating. People called him 'the lesbian's boyfriend'. Some assumed that I had simply gone through a phase. Others continued to attack me with homophobia. I continued to struggle with my sexuality, wondering if I really was gay, even as I dated a guy.

I ended up dropping out of school and I moved to Toronto at sixteen. I attended a small alternative school for kids who has been driven out of the mainstream school system due to homophobia. I was full of hope that I would finally be home, finally be accepted by queer community. Except, at the time, I had a boyfriend. I was also femme. So what I experienced was biphobia from the queer community, including the teachers at the school. I was not 'really queer' even after I started dating a girl at the school. The biphobia I experienced was nothing like the outright violent homophobia of my hometown. It was much more subtle, often communicated in looks, gestures, subtle comments, assumptions, and ways in which I was not included. Bisexuality also felt like an add on. It was not the central queer identity.

Eventually I came to accept myself as bisexual and as femme. And I realized that navigating the world in these identities meant experiencing both sexualized homophobic violence from heterosexual men, and biphobic dismissal in the queer communities which I wanted to call home. Biphobia also took the form of sexual violence from queer women who expected me to 'prove' my queerness by having sex with them, or who told me I 'wouldn't want men anymore' after having sex with them.

I came to like the word 'bisexuality' because it named my specific experience of biphobia. It named the experiences I have as a queer person who dates multiple genders, who experiences both homophobia and biphobia, who experiences a sense of not belonging in queer spaces. I came to like the word 'bisexuality' because it names my attraction for genders which are similar to mine and genders which are different from my own. I came to like the word 'bisexuality' because I knew how hated it was. I knew that bisexual femmes like myself were seen as 'asking for attention' and 'not really queer', narratives which have sexually violent undertones. I came to embrace it because it was hard won for me to accept that I am really queer, and that I do really have desire and attraction toward multiple genders.

Years passed and I continued to identify as bi. Something started to change though. The subtle dismissal of bisexuality started to take a more overt form. This new form was the accusation that bisexuality reinforced the gender binary. Every single time I came out as bi, or bisexuality was brought up, I heard queers insisting that bisexuality enforced a gender binary and erased trans identities. At first, I disagreed with this. I was not out as nonbinary yet, but I did know that my gender was fluid, and I did not experience bisexuality as an insistence on two discrete genders. But eventually, because I heard this critique so often, I gave up. I dropped 'bisexual' and started to identify as just 'queer'.

I identified this way for a few years and in that time I came out as nonbinary. Only recently have I begun to reconsider my rejection of bisexuality. Reading the work of bi activists really spoke to my experience. I felt seen and recognized in a way that I don't in general queer spaces and texts. My experiences of homophobia, biphobia, sexual violence from both straight men and queer women, the erasure of my nonbinary identity, my attraction toward multiple genders, and my history of relationships with people of multiple genders suddenly felt seen, remembered, validated. I began to question whether the insistence that bisexuality reinforces the gender binary is really just biphobia in disguise.

There are a whole bunch of statistics around bisexuals experiencing high rates of sexual violence, intimate partner violence, and suicide attempts. I don't have the study on hand, but I have read these statistics a number of times. I always found it striking because it really describes my experience but I didn't know what these experiences had to do with my bisexuality. I still don't know. I think it's a constellation of things, including the sexual violence bisexual people often experience, inside and outside of queer spaces, and the lack of a sense of belonging and community. I ran from homophobia only to find I had no safe place to land. The word 'bisexual' describes that experience in a way that 'queer' doesn't.

I am finding my way back to bisexuality as a queer nonbinary femme genderfluid person. I do not believe that bisexuality reinforces the gender binary. For me the 'bi' in 'bisexual' refers to attraction toward genders similar to my own and genders different from my own, which can shift and change depending on how I am embodying my gender. I am at a stage in my life where I am unearthing and working through the shame which has embedded in my body from a life time of sexual violence, including homophobic and biphobic violence. Part of this work, for me, is reclaiming bisexuality.

Social Isolation

I isolate a lot. The thing is that being around people exhausts me. I am extremely hypervigilant. I see threat everywhere. My worries aren't just worries they are cortisol corroding my insides. My level of fear is disproportionate with what is really going on. I wish it wasn't still like this. I wish there was an easy way out of it. I have longed for community, chosen family, friendship, for as long as I can remember. I have struggled with jealousy and resentment watching others make it look so easy. Hanging out with friends is supposed to help you relax but for me it is the opposite. It is stressful. So, I spend a lot of time alone. A lot of time avoiding people. I have a small number of close friends and we hang out from time to time. It takes me a long time to build up trust. Hanging out in groups of people is terribly overwhelming. I don't feel comfortable in my own skin and I don't know how to act or what to say. I put on personas in order to relieve the anxiety but these exhaust me and they are fake. I want this to be different, I really do.

But this is the way it is right now. Sometimes I try to 'fake it till I make it' and I end up making myself sick. So, I am trying to just be okay with where I am. I am trying to take small, manageable steps, like keeping in touch with the friends I do have. And I am working on my recovery, hoping to get to the root of it. Hoping that by taking care of myself, by working on feeling safer in my own skin, I will one day I will be able to come out of my shell. I am tired of feeling so alone. I am tired of being unable to have close friendship and community. I hate the fact that intimacy makes my skin crawl but it does. I keep hoping things will change, get easier, and maybe they will.

Trees

Looking at the trees, I wonder why I don't know their names. I realize it is because no one taught me. My parents did not teach me the names of the trees. I wonder why. I realize it is because no one taught them. Thinking this, my heart is a tumble of bricks. I realize, no one taught them about safety, bodily autonomy, or healthy relationships either. They couldn't teach me these things because they didn't know.

I think of my mother, a child. I think of my father, a child. My parents are both survivors of abuse, including sexual abuse. My parents, like myself, are powerless over the effects of trauma. They didn't know better, so they could not do better.

As I start the process of grieving all that was lost, I feel grief for my parents emerging. I know I need to grieve for myself, for my own losses. But I am also flooded with an awareness of intergenerational trauma. Pain upon pain upon pain.

Gender and Madness

I am genderfluid and nonbinary. For me this means that I experience my gender in a lot of different, changing ways, and that I don't experience my gender wholly within a male/female binary. I do experience binary genders as a part of my gender, but not all the time. When I first came out as genderqueer I was going by mixed pronouns. I would usually say they or she, and he if I was obviously presenting masc, which was rare. But, I got this sense that by saying they or she that people didn't really take me seriously as nonbinary. Even though I felt like being a woman was on some level a part of my gender, I felt like I had to leave that behind in order to be truly believed as a nonbinary person, and also, in order to have people use they pronouns for me. After awhile I started to get so fed up that I was only called they by other nonbinary people. So I started going by they all the time and insisting on it. It was really awful and frustrating and I have had a lot of bad experiences.

One of the biggest issues I have had has been trying to get a trans competent therapist. My partner also uses they/them pronouns and so do a lot of people I know. So I explained this all to my therapist and she said she could handle it and then couldn't. I ended up going through multiple therapists this way. Each one saying they could do it and then just not doing it. So I would leave and try to find another therapist. It was extremely annoying. And also just fucked and emotionally exhausting to start doing the work with these therapists and then having to leave because they couldn't handle they pronouns. Also I was paying these therapists. These weren't free services.

Insisting on they pronouns was so hard and I could tell I wasn't really taken seriously. Because I dress femme, so clearly I'm not trans right? That's the vibe I was getting and I could tell they thought it wasn't worth the effort to try. I would correct them each time they messed up someone's pronouns including my own. But, through this process, I also realized how much I had been forced to simplify my own gender in order to be taken seriously as a nonbinary person. Like, I would correct them when they called my child-self a girl, asking them to use child or kid. But sometimes I do think of my child self as a girl. And sometimes I don't.

Then the more complicated thing became clear to me. I haven't told anyone this because I fear not being taken seriously in my gender, and I fear that my changing relationship to gender and pronouns is annoying. I experience structural dissociation. Which means that my personality is split. I have two main splits and then a whole bunch of less elaborated ones which are based more on emotional states/emotional flashbacks. The two main splits are called Violet and Indigo. I don't talk about this much because I feel like people don't understand it. But I have had these splits since I was a kid and I gave them names when I was in high school. They have very different wants, desires, values, hopes, dreams, coping strategies, etc. Since getting sober Indigo has mainly run the show and Violet has become a scapegoat. I have been repressing Violet. Trying almost to eliminate... her.

So here's the thing. Violet uses she/her pronouns. She just does. Whenever I think of her these are the pronouns I use. When I would do this in therapy I would see this little flicker in the therapist's eyes like "See! You really do use she/her, you really are a woman, all this pronoun stuff is nonsense" etc. At least that's the way it felt. Like they felt that I was messing up on my own pronouns so therefore they didn't need to try to learn to use they/them. So I would try to avoid pronouns when talking about Violet. Or I would try to use they/them. But it felt wrong. And I eventually had to admit to myself that Violet uses she/her and Indigo uses they/them. They are both nonbinary because I am nonbinary. They are both genderfluid because I am genderfluid. But they experience these things in different ways.

I feel like there's no point in trying to explain this anyone. It brings up all the feels about being crazy and about being 'not trans enough'. But I am writing it down anyway. I guess, as of right now, I still want most people to use they/them for me, because the fact is that I am coercively gendered female in most spaces and called she all the time. But maybe for those who are close to me and who truly get this or think they might be able to get, they can use a mix of they and she.

Gender and madness mixed together make things more complicated.

What I Can't Say

What is this time travel? What are these dreams? Why am I stricken by love, helpless? Grief comes in waves they say. Sneaks up unexpected. Suddenly, I can't move. I can't tell the truth. I can't say anything. Because I have already lost everything.

I wonder how many different ways I can say it. How many poems I can write. How many songs. I wonder how much cryptic writing I can write to simultaneously express and hide the truth.

It comes out nowhere, soft like a flood. The shape of dreams. My mouth cupped over the sound of an amends. I want to say: *You meant so much to me. I am sorry. I forgive you.*

I want words to release us, to heal us, to mend us. I want a way out of what happened. I want another ending. I don't want the unbelievable truth to be the truth but it is. I have spent so long finding ways to accept it. Keeping it maintained like a hard line so I don't die.

But I'm under water in the sweetness of sleep and I remember other things. I remember you were kind to me. I remember your smile. I remember the joy, the peace, the presence. The way I felt with you. The way we were together.

It wasn't all terror. It wasn't all damage. But it was enough of both to be deadly. I have repeated the truth. I could die. You could kill me if I let you. I have memorized the impact of my arm and the beam as I went through the wall.

But under the water, deep down in the dream, I remember your laugher, us riding bikes together, how happy I was. These memories come to me still. All these years later.

I wish I could say I miss you, but I know that everyone would say I'm insane.

(I want to erase this and not publish it. I want to come forward all calm and collected and say that I don't engage in this sort of thinking anymore, than I am so over it, that I don't romanticize people who try to kill me. But, well, things are complicated. Feelings are complicated. I don't totally understand it. I don't know why these feelings still come over me years later. I don't know if I can call it love. bell hooks says that love and abuse can't coexist and reading that changed my life, gave me something to hope for. But the feelings that I have for the person who abused me, who I believed I loved, who is also a survivor, well, they are complicated. And sometimes, rarely these days, but sometimes, these feelings of sadness and love come over me. I could pretend I don't have these feelings because they aren't the 'right' feelings to have, but the truth is, sometimes I still do.)

Graveyard

Sometimes my sexuality feels like a graveyard. Just bones. Dust and bones.

Sometimes the nothingness has a surge of energy. Oh my god, there is want underneath, but it is just like a ghost.

Haunting. My sexuality is haunting me.

I want to rip off my skin. Get a new body. Not have a body at all.

I want to remember my body, come back in. I want to feel these pulses that rise like waves. I want to feel again. I can't feel anything.

Sometimes my sexuality feels like a graveyard. I am a ghost. I can't get over it no matter how hard I try.

I plant the seeds but the earth has been soured here.

I feel like I'm dying as soon as I open my eyes.

Magic at my fingertips. Magic when I remember. But I can't remember my body.

I am terrified of walking into that storm.

It feels like the sound of a sob. I don't know if there's an end to the nothingness or the pain it is covering.

I don't know if the dead can rot and create new life.

I don't know if there's a way back to my body.

I don't know if there's a way to feel again.

The Mushroom Patch

There used to be a mushroom patch down the street from my house. Every time I passed it I would stop to look at all those beauties pushing up from the soil, clustering around a tree trunk. Then one day, the mushroom patch was gone. Some people cut it down when they cut the grass.

This summer I have been depressed. Sometimes urgently and deeply. Sometimes just slowly, under the surface. I am sad and I am lonely. I am isolating because people stress me out, because I am jealous, because I feel like people really don't want me around.

I was having a bad morning, woke up in deep depression. I walked out into my backyard and I saw that a mushroom patch had sprung up overnight. A big beautiful mushroom patch. I was elated. My spirits were lifted. My heart opened and extended. I was filled with joy.

I showed my partner the mushroom patch. We marveled at it. In a couple days the mushroom caps started opening up. It was wonderful to see.

The city owns the house I live in and they send workers to cut the grass in the backyard. One morning in my bedroom I heard the lawnmower and I was filled with dread. I knew they were going to cut down the mushroom patch.

After the worker left I rushed into the backyard to see mushroom bodies lying all across the ground. The whole mushroom patch was killed. I felt awful.

When my partner got home I told them what happened and they asked why I didn't go out and tell the worker not to cut down the mushroom patch. I felt sick when I heard this. That had not seemed like a possibility to me. I did not know I could do that. Now that this was presented to me I felt complicit in the death of the mushroom patch.

I have such a hard time standing up for myself, setting boundaries, asking for what I want. I grew up in an environment where I was punished for resisting sexual abuse. And this is what it has done to me. I was devastated that I had not stood up for and protected the mushroom patch.

Later I talked to my sponsor from a 12 step program that deals with the effects of growing up in dysfunctional homes. I told her that I felt so guilty and responsible and that I hadn't stood up for what I love. I loved the mushroom patch and it is so difficult and dangerous to love.

She reminded me that I am powerless. I am powerless over the effects of trauma, until I heal, until I develop a spiritual connection that will give me other options. I can't do better when I don't know better. I can't hold myself up to others who were not sexually abused and expect myself to act like them.

I have to forgive myself for not protecting the mushroom patch. I have to grieve the mushroom patch. I have to work on my healing and trust that as I heal, I will become able to stand up for the mushroom patch (if it is able to grow back), myself, my values, and those I care about.

But it takes time. Even though I have four years of sobriety from drugs and alcohol I am just beginning to address the impacts of childhood trauma. I am doing my best and more will be revealed with time.

I am frozen inside. Intimacy is so difficult for me. But I loved that mushroom patch. That mushroom patch melted my heart. I just didn't know how to put the love into action.

Submerged, Emerging

I haven't been able to write or even speak. Life has continued onward, beautiful things have unfolded, but some part of myself has dropped out of the picture, submerged, emerging, I have been ignoring a voice that cannot form words.

I have never been able to do the same thing forever. I have always had to do something else. I have never been able to sustain motivation under the intention of 'goodness'. I can't 'be good'. I can't 'write good writing'. Nothing I do will have any meaning if I start from a place of trying to be good.

But all I want is to be good.

I don't want to write about child abuse. I don't want to feel like a fish on a hook or a fish in a bucket, mouth moving, eyes wide. I don't want to feel this weight like endless water that is still here, still inside me somehow.

I don't want to write out what was done to me, to point fingers of righteous indignation at parents I still can't bring myself to blame.

I want to curl up in a closet. I want a body like a stone. I want to disappear beneath the water never to return.

I can't tell the truth about any of it, because the truth is an alienating, painful mess.

I'm researching dissociation and I start to dissociate. I am reading about the impact child abuse has on brain development. I am reading about symptoms of complex trauma: migraines, autoimmune disorders, forgetfulness, confusion, persistent dysphoria, suicide attempts, self injury, alcoholism, digestion issues, derealization, depersonalization, inability to form close relationships, compulsive sexuality, no sexuality... and on and on. My life, my body, my mind, all the things I can't change no matter how hard I try.

I am tired of talking about it, tired of writing about it, tired of thinking about it, tired of it in my body, tired of it on my tongue, tired of it all crammed up in the wordless places, tired of it in my dreams.

I am almost thirty now. Not a child for quite some time. But it gets more real every day.

I am tired of talking about it but I want you to *know*.

There is such a thing as emotional sexual abuse.

There is such a thing as implicit incest.

I get triggered. I get into compulsive telling. The memories cascade into one another. They are linked like a web. Each trauma unfolds into another one. The urgency pushes forward. I must tell you, because I need you to understand.

I tell you about my childhood. My father, my grandfather.

I tell you about the drinking years, the show where I was given blunt force trauma in my arm that killed my nerves there, the stairs I was dragged down.

I tell you about the nameless, faceless guys, the years of rape never quite called rape.

I try to count. I have never been able to count. I stop counting.

I tell you about him, Ashton.

I am bewildered with the telling and my body becomes like a weight I am somehow attached to. I haven't been here for a very long time.

Suicide

Secret: I am 29 years old and I still think about suicide all the time. It follows me, follows me like the ghost of my grandfather, not the grandfather who sexually assaulted me, the one who jumped off a bridge and took his own life, forever changing the lives of those who love him, years before I was born.

I have intrusive thoughts. Over and over and over. *I give up. I can't do this anymore. You may not want to kill yourself but you are going to.* Some of the thoughts aren't words, but visions, feelings. My arms ache for knives. I don't mean to sound cliché, but I never got over my fifteen year old angst. It is still with me. So much of the time, suicide calls, not as a way into death, but as a way out of life, out of this life which weighs so heavy with pain.

I have tried already. Bottles of pills, passing out in full bathtubs with my nose just above the surface, waking up in cold black water, alive. I have already drank the charcoal, not the trendy detox charcoal lemonade but the 'Drink this', 'What is it?', 'Chocolate milk', choking down thick gritty black filth, constipated and shitting black in the psych ward. I have already been formed. I have already said my prayers and thanked whoever was listening for another shot at life. I have already tried again and I have already given up again.

I have already put myself in all the dangerous situations: train bridges, the medium in the middle of a six lane highway, strangers' cars, strangers' apartments, park benches, big mouth and bad consequences. I have burned up with a desire for life, for living, pushing through me with all the fervor of the suicidal. Obsession with lakes, rocks in pockets. Lying on bathroom floors, eyes to the ceiling.

I have been bottle free for four years, razor free for two. I don't overdose or stare at traffic wondering how bad I feel about taking others with me anymore. My suicidal thoughts, heavy and weighted, play out in the background, insistent, persistent, but ignored. I keep trying. Looking for that right therapist. Looking for that right prayer, that right magic. Remembering all the days I am grateful it never worked. Seeking solace in small things. Finding what happiness I can.

I will live. I will grow old. I have seen my hands age before my eyes during a drug-fueled trip, becoming the soft, wrinkled hands of the old. I have appeared to another in a vision, fleeting, but I was without a doubt, an elder. I will not take my life.

I may never be happy. *You will never be happy.*

I might.

Never Been Queer

Four years sober and I am only beginning to scratch the surface of the trauma that fractured my personality. Four years sober and I am just beginning to address the chronic health issues which stem from years of excess cortisol, tension, inflammation. Trauma stored in my flesh and muscle, in my neural pathways, my guts, my skin. Four years sober and I am only just beginning to see the extent of the damage done, the weight of intergenerational trauma. I am only just beginning to understand that it really was that bad, that it's not just that I'm 'crazy'. I'm not making it up.

So much of it was subtle, or it seemed subtle because it was so normal. For so long I did not know to call what happened to me 'sexual abuse'. My grandfather forced his tongue into my mouth when I was twelve, held me against my will in his arms and made out with me. That was the only actual assault. Except for what my family called 'slippery slobberies', in which he grabbed us and rubbed his mouth and tongue forcefully against our faces, without penetrating the mouth. But that was normal in my family. And we were yelled at, called disrespectful and ungrateful, if we tried to resist.

So much I don't remember. Large, yawning blanks of nothingness. I know my father screamed at us all the time. But I don't remember most of it. A few memorable pieces stand out. Being called a 'selfish pig' for example. Most of it is just implied in my memories, implied by the way my family referred to it as the 'big voice', by the fragments of memories. My mother frantically telling my father 'don't' as he insisted on screaming at the driver who had cut him off to 'pull over'. There's so much I don't remember and so much I can't say.

I came into my queerness in the context of violence. Sexual violence warps the mind. I experienced my own developing sexuality with terror, shame, and disgust. When I discovered that my sexuality was the 'wrong' kind, this deepened my shame. I felt disgusting. This combined with the subtle and outright messages of homophobia and heterosexism made me hate myself for being queer, even as I yearned for a life where I could be. When I came out of the closet at 14, I was called a dyke every day, told I was disgusting and going to burn in hell. Guys yelled 'something smells like fish' when I walked by. My friends told me not to look at them when they changed. They pulled away abruptly if I touched them. I was looked upon with suspicion, asked questions like 'if you're gay, does that mean you are sexually attracted to yourself?'

I go to therapy and recount the stories, preparing for EMDR, treatment which I desperately need and have been trying to access for years. I tell the stories but I don't feel anything. Sometimes I feel sick and my body becomes a dead weight and everything is filled with space: space between my eyes and the back of my skull, space between the words in my sentences, space between one thought and the next.

I have never been able to be queer. I have never been able to exist inside my body, inside my sexuality, safely and fully. Trauma and addiction took that from me. Deep shame, terror, and disgust implanted through sexual violence and homophobia have made my body and sexuality unsafe. I have dissociated from them. Whether it was the compulsive sex with men during my active addiction or my inability to really connect with my sexuality in sobriety, whether it's my lack of sex drive or the fact that I have never been able to truly express desire for a woman without feeling like I'm disgusting, whether it's the fact that I can't settle into my body without immediately feeling unsafe or that I am plagued with jealousy and fear of abandonment, sexual violence has robbed me of so much. I am only just beginning to realize that homophobia is, in and of itself, a form of sexual violence.

Four years sober and recovery is a full time job again. I'm almost 30 and I believe that I should be healthier by now, have it more together. Instead I am juggling naturopath and acupuncture appointments, multiple 12 step fellowships, therapy, a gym membership, and mood swings which are not actually mood swings, they are structural dissociation manifesting itself. I feel like I am climbing uphill only to keep slipping backwards. I am sick and tired of being sick and tired and I am sober. I am doing everything I need to do, everything I can, while I can, until I can't, and then I start again. I try again.

I dream of a time when I will finally feel safe, safe in my body, safe in community, safe in relationships, safe in my sexuality, safe in my queerness. Sobriety has planted the seeds of hope that this might be possible. Sometimes the hope is an unstoppable flood, sometimes it is a flickering flame. Often it still feels impossible but I keep trying because I still have hope. I dream of a time when I can be fully alive, fully here, in my body, in my being, in my queerness, in my sobriety. I want to embody my queerness fully, to exist completely embodied in all that was stolen from me. I want to be really queer, completely queer, alive in my queerness, unashamed and unafraid of all that I am.

Denial

I am going through massive change right now.

Denial is a skill which I have perfected. It comes as naturally as breathing. I learned it well as a child, because denial is how my family operates, and denial was necessary to survive.

For a long time I have been isolated and depressed. I have felt ambivalent and indecisive. I have been unable to commit to the many changes I have tried to implement in my life. I have felt stuck. And lost.

I couldn't put my finger on what was wrong. I couldn't exactly articulate it. But it was like a ball and chain around my ankle. Something. Something slowing me down, holding me back, sinking me.

I came out of denial suddenly and violently. My whole being was shaken by what was revealed to me.

I am forced to face the ways that I survive by being dishonest with myself.

I am returning to myself, to my recovery, to my feelings, to the process. Layer by layer, I face the truth.

The effects of trauma can be both obvious and subtle at the same time. Sneaky, ubiquitous, pervasive. Again and again I come back around and find another way that I am living in sickness rather than solution. I don't judge myself for this because I know that these skills have kept me alive.

But at this point in my life I want something different.

I am Not Who I Swore I Was

Who am I now that the lies are gone? Now that denial has slipped through my fingers? Who am I now that I'm not hungry for love, looking, searching, make believing, imagining, insisting, putting up with everything? Who am I now that I am big enough to love the child that I am, big enough and strong enough to hold that child, love that child, comfort that child, *protect* that child? Who am I now that I no longer care what you think of me? Who am I now that I don't need your approval, desperately, relentlessly? Who am I now that my memories fall like feathers, now that I accept each one with kindness, now that I finally, finally take my own hand? I'm not an archetype. I am not a role model. I am not a hero. I am not a cool and popular person. I am not a fuckable thing. I am not who you wanted me to be. I am not who I swore I was. I am something else and that something else exists in the folding and unfolding, the way that reality materializes in the magic of finally seeing, seeing what has always existed, deep in the seed, as pure potentiality.

Betrayal

I can't pretend anymore.
Pretend that I am happy.
Pretend that it is all okay.
Pretend that this is what I deserve.
All I deserve.
Pretend it's my fault or my responsibility.
Pretend that I don't want so much more.
Hunger for it.
Pretend that betrayal isn't boring.
Pretend that betrayal isn't something I already know.

Body

I can no longer ignore my physical body. I have been ignoring my body for so long. Dissociative. Leaving my body. Surviving somewhere up in the sky. For years I abused my body, because it was the only way I knew how to survive. I barely ate. I spent days puking my guts out. I coughed up black resin from my lungs all the time. I drank and drank and drank. After getting sober, I started binge eating, using food where alcohol used to be.

I have also put so much of my self worth into my body as a sex object, a tool, a form of currency, to get what I thought I needed, which was some kind of attention, which I used in place of genuine care. I was never well enough to really care for body, attend to my body. My body became a thing. Objectified and abandoned. A means to an end or not really there at all. I was so dissociative that I didn't even notice how sick I was. Only when obliterating pain sent me to the emergency room. Otherwise I was comfortably in denial.

Now, at four years sober, I can't ignore it anymore. I want to come back into my body. Somehow. I want to learn how to care for my body. How to be kind to my body. I want to get at the root of the sickness, all the chronic sickness, which I know is literally trauma, physically, materially here in my body.

I have started seeing a naturopath. She thinks I have SIBO (small intestine bacterial overgrowth), which would explain a lot. She asked me if I ever had food poisoning. I said no. She asked me if I've ever thrown up a lot. Yes. Alcoholism. Well, apparently that can cause bacteria from the large intestine to come up into the small intestine where it causes all sorts of problems. I took a test and I'm waiting for the results.

I started going for acupuncture. The acupuncturist told me my symptoms are the classic case of sexual trauma. The needles go in and I lie in the chair. I am trying to be kind to my body. I go for a massage once a month. The massage therapist told me I wear my shoulders like earrings. There is so much pain from all the tension.

I am learning about herbs and making my own tinctures using apple cider vinegar. I am brewing strong tea. I am trying to be patient. It is difficult. I am tired of feeling sick. I am embarrassed by the issues my body is having. It affects my self esteem and my ability to show up in my life.

But I am taking steps now. I am addressing it rather than ignoring it, and that is good. It took a long time for things to get like this, a slow accumulation of trauma and damage, so I need to be patient with my recovery. Patient and consistent. I am doing my best.

I joined the gym. The Y has a geared-to-income rate. I was super nervous and afraid to go, but slowly I have started to love it. The feeling of my body. Of moving my body. For myself. Not as a performance. Not for someone else's eyes. Not for someone else's desire. My body moving and sweating and growing stronger. It feels really good.

Sexuality is the other thing and it honestly makes me want to cry. I have almost no access to my sexuality and sometimes I don't care, but right now I do. I wish I could feel. I wish I could access my desire without feeling shame or terror. I wish I wish I wish.

I have been trying little things. Reading erotica but not really being into it. Watching shipping videos on youtube which I am into. I am going to be going to these weekly meetings about overcoming sexual self-hatred and I am looking forward to that.

I want to heal. Really. I want to feel whole and good and safe and complete. I want access to all of who I am. I want to come back into my body for real.

I am tired of what sexual violence has done to me.

Blood, Bone, Muscle

Once a week I go to a recreational boxing class for survivors of violence. On the first week I cried. I didn't know how to punch. I felt so weak against the weight of the heavy bag. I remembered his weight on top of me. His laughter when I tried to fight back. How ridiculous it was that I could even try to defend myself. My submission. My inevitable submission.

But I came back. I began to feel the strength in my body as I gained skill. I lost myself in the drills, unable to think anything, all body and impact, all fist. No words, no doubts, no memories. No fears or wants or worries. Just impact. Power. Punch. Jab. Punch.

I leave class and I feel different in my body. I hold my head higher, my spine no longer curling in on myself. I know my body more intimately than I did before. My body the animal, warm, flesh, blood. Bone. Muscle. My body not as dead thing, lifeless thing, reduced to nothing. My body not as weight, relentless weight, pulling down my abstract disembodied thoughts. My body as real. As myself. As movement, power, feeling. Connected. Here. Home. Am.

I walk or ride and I watch the sun come down over the cityscape. I feel like if someone tried something I would at least have a chance. I feel like for the first time in my life 'fight' is an option. Not just flight, or more like, freeze, submit.

The abject terror of submission isn't everything, isn't all I know. There is something else. Some secret truth in my fist, connected to my wrist, a power moving from some centre I didn't know I had. My body no longer abandoned, my body returning to life.

Solstice Magic

A new light enters my life. The seed of a flame incubated in darkness. The longest night and the brightest light together create powerful magic. The darkness is surrender and also the deep earth which feeds the seed. The darkness is rich with possibility and ending. It hides and reveals mysteries. The fire burns away, cleanses, destroys. It brings the warmth of the heart, the heat of the blood. The darkness and the fire both destroy and keep us alive. The darkness is an absence of warmth. The fire heats us up. The darkness is the space of possibility. The fire burns to the ground.

Tonight I felt myself being reborn. My Saturn has returned. 30 is just around the corner. My feet froze in my boots as I stood next to my dear friend in a crowd full of strangers and neighbors watching fire throwers and people wearing masks, hearing the beating of drums. My body ached for the fire and when they lit the ouroboros I felt the power of watching it burn. We all moved a little closer to the flame feeling it warm our icy bodies. We all stood in awe as the fire consumed, destroyed, revealed. The night was lit up and ablaze. So were our hearts. I am no longer who I used to be.

The light guides the way through the darkness. I follow the light. I soak up the darkness. I am honoured by both. Grateful for both. I light the candles on my altar to feed the energy further. I feel the fire in my heart, the fire of transformation. I surrender to solstice magic, knowing I am exactly where I need to be. All of the lies burn away, all of the false hope and pretending succumbs to the flame. The heat stirs deep desires and I remember who I am. I lay down my tarot cards to make tangible what I've learned. I ask the questions. I surrender the answers.

The lesson is the Five of Wands. The lesson is to stop trying to run the show, to stop trying to meet my needs through little plans and designs. The lesson is that I can't force it. I can't make something be which isn't meant to be. The lesson is that I don't need to prove my worth. I don't need to convince, contrive, struggle, try so hard. What is next is the Hanged Man: surrender. That deep, most powerful magic of letting go. By the brightest light and longest darkness I turn over my will and my life to the care of the Universe. I have absolute trust. I have absolute faith. Control is unnecessary. What is meant to be will most certainly be. I let myself flow into the power of something so much greater than me. Who I'm becoming is someone entirely new, the Queen of Wands. I am growing up, growing into my skin. I let go of old stories I tell myself about myself. I am confident, social, and assured. I no longer look to others to validate me or provide me with self worth. I am safe and secure in my being. I like who I am.

Darkness and light, fire and cold, power and possibility, surrender and transformation. With a full heart, with utter gratitude, I pass through the longest night surrounded by flame.

Conclusion

This book ends with everything falling apart. In a way it circles back to the beginning, a time of hitting rock bottom and deep desperation, a recognition that things need to change. Healing is like that, cyclical. We go deeper and more is revealed as we become ready to face it.

The life I built in sobriety came crashing to the ground at the end of 2016. Deep in trauma work, I came out of denial about the fact that my long term partnership was deeply harmful to me. My whole world and the careful web of lies I had built to hide the truth from myself fell to the ground.

But just like with the beginning of sobriety I found the willingness to fight for my life. I stayed sober and I worked hard to get out and to create a new life. I felt like I was dying but I was really being reborn.

I want to end this book by telling you that 2017 was the best year of my life thus far. I reconnected with my body, with my power, with my sexuality, with my joy. I followed my heart and my dreams and things became possible which I never would have believed were possible. I changed profoundly and completely. The work of change continues, but wow, I don't even recognize my life, it is so profoundly different.

Healing is fucking real and sometimes things are hardest right before they begin to change. Wherever you are in your journey, hold on. Don't give up. I promise you, things can change.

More will be revealed. Magic is real. Change is possible. Hope is brave. And all the hard work is so, so worth it.

I believe in your magic. I believe in you.

Clementine

Acknowledgements

Thank you to all of those who traveled the path of recovery with me during these five years, especially my fellow alcoholics and addicts, my fellow trauma survivors, and my queer and trans communities. Thank you to the 12 step communities in Toronto that literally saved my life. Thank you to Montréal 12 step communities, and to RadSob, for helping me to reconnect with my recovery. Thank you to all the zinesters keeping zine culture alive and thriving. Thank you to all the people who support, believe in, and follow my work. Thank you for reading this.

Thank you to my friends, loved ones, and community: Jordyn Taylor, Jasmin Fahd, Casey Jean, Amy Saunders, Ash Baksi, Holly Jo, Nicole Davis, Stephanie Creaghan, Rebecca Woodmass, Leigh Hoffman, Alex Felicitas, Renée Yoxon, Gustavo Guzman, Emily Macdonald, Kelsey Blair, Tommi Parrish, Kelsey Traikov, D.J. Fraser, Elina Shnayderman, Cacie Prins, Evelyn Ricky, and Jay Marquis-Manicom, to name only a few. A very special thank you to Jay for showing me what real love looks like and helping me in the work of repairing so much of the damage that was done to me.

This work was written on Wendat, Anishinaabe, and Haudenosaunee land, known as Tkaronto/Toronto. I am currently living on unceded Kanien'keha:ka territory known as Tiohtià:ke/ Montréal.

C LEMENTINE MORRIGAN is a writer, poet, rebel scholar, and working witch. She writes the zine *Fucking Magic*. Their first book, *Rupture*, was published in 2012. Her second collection of poetry, *The Size of a Bird*, was published in 2017. Their creative writing has appeared in the literary journals *Prose & Lore* and *Soliloquies*, and her scholarly writing has appeared in the academic journals *Somatechnics, The Canadian Journal of Disability Studies,* and *Knots*. They have also written for *Guts Magazine* and *Shameless Magazine*. She is the creator of two short films, *Resurrection* (2013) and *City Witch* (2016). Their creative, artistic, and scholarly works consider trauma, madness, addiction, sobriety, gender, sexuality, desire, queerness, polyamory, kink, magic, re-enchantment, environment, and more-than-human worlds. She facilitates workshops and guest lectures on a number of topics. They provide professional tarot reading services for individuals and events. She is a white settler of Irish, Scottish, and English ancestry living on unceded Kanien'keha:ka territory. They are a practitioner of trauma magic. For more of her work visit clementinemorrigan. com or follow them on instagram @clementinemorrigan.